FROM THE PRODL

MW01033829

Conquering Hollywood

The Screenwriter's Blueprint for Career Success

Gary W. Goldstein

Bigger Picture Press
Los Angeles, California

Conquering Hollywood
The Screenwriter's Blueprint for Career Success

Copyright © 2013 Gary W. Goldstein

Published 2013 by Bigger Picture Press
Santa Monica, California

For information about bulk order special discounts
Please contact Bigger Picture Press
www.ConqueringHollywood.com

First Edition July 2013

ISBN 978-0-9897152-0-1

Published And Printed In The United States Of America

Book Cover Design by David Kessler
Layout Design by Thomas White

To my dad, who encouraged me to follow my intuition, find my true gifts and, above all, be happy.

ACKNOWLEDGEMENTS

One name goes on the book, yet many contributed. To all who generously shared their time, invaluable insights and counsel throughout the writing of this book, I'm deeply grateful.

To J.F. Lawton, Allison Burnett, Richard Hatem, Ilana Bar-Din, Bob Berlinger, Jon Bernstein and the many others who entrusted to me either the management of their career or the responsibility of producing their projects, it's an honor to act as steward of another's creativity and I'm humbled and thankful.

A galactic 'thank you' to my editor, Jeanne McCafferty. Ever-gracious, unyielding in her enthusiasm, fiercely smart, unfailingly thorough, Jeanne educated me every step of the way. This book fulfills its promise in large measure thanks to Jeanne who is impeccable, ever-patient, gently honest, unwilling to settle.

To my friends, inspirations, teachers, mentors and role models who make a big beautiful dent in my universe, I treasure your counsel and friendship. In particular, Adam Linter, a friend who taught me much and who left too soon. Grace Breuer, who's been my Gibraltar and whose steadfast belief has sustained me through many a challenge. And Morgan Agnes Carson, a friend whose joyful creativity, heart and contribution are a gift beyond measure.

Michael Margolis, Jonathan Fields, Peter Hoppenfeld, Michael Fishman, Jim Kwik, Tommy Bahler - friends, brothers, mentors, each of whom is a bold adventurer and deeply committed to extraordinary works of great service. All big brilliant stars in the constellation of my life, each of whom adds a dimension to my understanding and joy. Some people just make you play a better game.

I've no doubt overlooked and forgotten to name many that deserve mention, either for their contribution to this book or simply for the exquisite pleasure of and lessons learned from our friendships.

And to an early hero, Maxwell E. Perkins, who inspired me to leave a perfectly good life as an attorney in San Francisco and run away to the circus! And, finally, to my greatest hero, my dad, who travelled an unimaginable distance and taught me more about life than I can put into words.

Gary W. Goldstein

Table of Contents

FOREWORD

by J.F. Lawton

(screenwriter)

"Pretty Woman", "Under Siege", "The Hunted"

When I first met Gary Goldstein, I had been struggling in Hollywood for five years, dreaming about becoming a screenwriter but getting nowhere. I had no agent, no manager, and no prospects for any. I worked odd jobs to pay the rent on a tiny apartment, off the end of Hollywood Boulevard, where hookers would pace up and down looking for customers. At the time, I was making money teaching more successful screenwriters how to use Macintosh computers for word processing. One recommended me to Gary to help him with his own computers.

I knew that Gary ran a management company for writers, but I was too nervous to ask him to help me. I needed the cash from his computer consulting gig and didn't want to bother him. But after I had finished my work on his new computer system, having heard I was a writer, he generously offered to read one of my scripts.

By that time, I had written a pile of different scripts and occasionally 'industry' people would agree to read them. But they rarely did. Because, frankly, reading a 120 page script is a pain in the ass for anyone who's busy. But I sent a script over to Gary in hopes that, this time, it would be different.

It was. Gary actually read it. He told me it was pretty good, but he wasn't looking for any more clients. But he thought maybe he could help me find someone else to represent me. Did I have any more scripts? I sent him another.

Gary read that one too, and thought it was interesting. But again, he wasn't looking for new clients. Did I have any more scripts? I did, but I wasn't sure what the point of him reading them was if he wasn't going to represent me. Still, I sent him a third script, thinking this was all a waste of our time.

The next time we met, not only had he read that third script, he said he wanted to represent me. He quickly explained how he worked. He took a commission off of any script that he sold, except for the ones that he produced himself. I was thrilled. Here was a person who could not only sell my scripts, but produce them. And he was smart enough not to sign me off of one script, but had read several to see if I was truly a good writer who could deliver. He signed me off of my writing alone, despite the fact that I had no credits and no prospects. I left thinking that with this powerful manager/producer's help, I would finally get a chance to make it in the industry.

And I was right. Within a few years, thanks to Gary, I had several movies produced, most by him, including a couple of box office smashes. One of them was about those hookers near my apartment. He became not only my manager, but my best friend.

However, when I look back on the day when Gary signed me as a client, I realize I forgot to ask a very important question.

What the hell have you done?

The answer, I would not fully realize until many successful years later, was: little.

Because at the time I met Gary, he hadn't produced any movies. He had just started his management company, and didn't have a clue about the business of Hollywood. He was just an ex-hippie lawyer who got bored with his old job and decided it might be fun to get into movies. This should have been obvious to me, because who the hell would waste their time reading three full scripts from some unknown writer?

I am, to this day, grateful that he did. In retrospect, it's probably better I didn't know that he knew nothing about the business. He certainly didn't let the fact that he knew nothing get in his way. And, as William Goldman famously said, this is a business where <u>nobody</u> knows anything.

After all these years, it's finally been my turn to read something that Gary has written. It's been a pleasure. Here is a book of practical advice for those seeking a career in Hollywood, written by someone who, at least now, really knows what the hell he's talking about. Maybe it isn't so true that nobody knows anything. Because I think Gary certainly does.

Conquering Hollywood

The Screenwriter's Blueprint for Career Success

INTRODUCTION: START YOUR ENGINES

I dare you to prove that you are more than you ever believed yourself to be. Dare to prove that there is more in you, more to you, that there is a dimension of you that the world has not seen. Dare to spread your wings, and soar, and sail.

~ Jack Boland, developer of the Master Mind Journal

You're serious about your talent and kicking your career in entertainment into a higher gear. I know this because you've just picked up this book and turned to this page.

By choosing this book, you've already distinguished yourself as being among the few who actively seek out information, strategies and tools to grow your career as a business.

Success in Hollywood is a choice. It's a set of habits, a mindset, a discipline and an action plan anyone can master. This book is designed so you know exactly, specifically and precisely what to do to gain advantage over your competitors who are *not* doing what it takes.

Experts in the business world hold varying opinions on many things, but they all claim marketing is the key to success for any career or enterprise (and likely responsible for as much as 90% of individual successes). Let's face it, the un-marketed career is a hobby.

Hollywood, like all of life and business, is not a meritocracy. Those who market themselves the smartest, the most effectively and the most frequently, are the ones who succeed. Period.

Talent comes second to marketing. If that weren't true, only those with extraordinary talent would succeed. If that weren't true, only high quality films and TV shows would get produced. But we know that's not the case. You likely have said to yourself on occasion, "I have more talent than so-and-so". Very likely you do. But the person with less talent whose work is up there on the big or small screen was fiercely determined and consistently dedicated to marketing themselves. They simply meant it and wanted it more. That's where the rubber meets the road.

CAREER, NOT CRAFT

Although this is a *how to* book dedicated to screenwriters, this book does not address screenwriting techniques or craft. There are many valuable teachers, seminars, books, webinars, CDs and DVDs dedicated to the art of writing screenplays. They can be found on Google or Amazon, or in any major bookstore.

This book teaches *career*. Screenwriting is a business, requiring business skills and a career plan. Your business model or career plan does not need to be lengthy or complex. In fact, simple is better, and easier to execute on a regular basis. It should be thoughtful, fun and something you're genuinely excited about and willing to do for yourself. You want a plan that embraces effective strategies for:

- marketing
- networking
- team-building, and becoming represented by an agent and/or manager
- developing a creative *signature*
- pitching
- getting your scripts read by the right people
- and more.

This book is your roadmap to success in Hollywood. Your *how to* guide. It is constructed so that after the introduction of a few essential business strategies, you will put those strategies into practice and that's when the *how-to* comes into play:

- How to gain access.
- How to get noticed.
- How to initiate relationships.
- How to adopt successful strategies to build a career in Hollywood.

So you can become a working professional in film and/or in television. And that's the point, isn't it?

Here's what this book is **not:**

- It is **not** about craft.
- It is **not** a collection of war stories.
- It is **not** from the point of view of a successful producer or other seasoned professionals in the entertainment business.

This book is from **your** point of view. It gives you the things you need to know to 'make it' in the competitive world of film and TV. The things you need to do, that anyone can do if you're serious and modestly disciplined. The things that will help you create your opportunity, create your break in the biz, and put you in the driver's seat of your career.

And being in the driver's seat of your career—whether you've just completed your first screenplay, or have been writing for years—means the freedom to abandon a day-job because you're earning income from your writing. Getting your screenplays optioned, purchased and produced is attainable! Getting on staff on a successful network or cable series is within your reach.

AN INSIDER'S EXPERIENCE

This book is a distillation of my experience in Hollywood and the savvy I've accumulated over the years.

As a literary manager and later as a producer, I've represented and collaborated with creative talent for 25 years. My focus and specialty has been newer or professionally younger talent. Initially, my own lack of experience dictated this as a practical matter. The excitement of discovering, championing and succeeding with and for younger writers inspired me to stay the course. Necessity motivated me to design and refine techniques to accelerate their success. Early on, I didn't have the luxury of taking years to transform a new writer with real talent (but with a scant or non-existent resume) into a revenue-generating client. The faster I launched careers, the more sense it made for all parties concerned, and it simply became habit to stick with a targeted handful of techniques that consistently delivered real-world, rapid results.

What you are about to learn are the identical strategies I used to transform non-working, newer talent into working talent with real careers. I even became my own client, transforming myself from talent representative to film producer. Well over one billion dollars in worldwide film revenues later, I'm proof of the success of this method. I put into practice every single strategy I describe in this book to grow not only the careers of many clients, but my own career in Hollywood.

These simple strategies worked for my clients, they worked for me personally, and they will work for you. In the majority of cases, my clients, like many of you reading this book, had no agent, no attorney, no team. They had a dream, and they had talent. They just needed a concrete, focused action plan to make it. So, if you want to distinguish yourself, make relationships, learn how to gain huge advantage over the thousands of other writers who are your competition, read on!

PUT IT IN WRITING

Starting with laser-focused strategies greatly magnifies your probability of success. *A written set of goals and a detailed plan for achieving those benchmarks is essential.*

Starting without a plan is a recipe for frustration, confusion and failure. You're competing toe-to-toe with countless established professionals and newer competition, with thousands more each year from all around the U.S. and beyond joining the ranks of those dreaming of breaking into *Hollywood.*

You wouldn't get in your car and set out to drive to a new distant destination without consulting a map -- and your career deserves more care, planning and effort than a casual road trip.

The confidence of having your own unique *success map* is the most valuable gift you can give your career. Each day, each week, each month, you know what to do and can actually measure how much closer you are to achieving each of your goals and desires.

Your success depends on one thing: preparation. Prepare a smart plan, study the strategies in this book, do the exercises, make a commitment to take action every day (even if only for 30 minutes), and you will increase tenfold your chances for success in Hollywood. The strategies in this book will open doors and create opportunities faster and faster the more you take action.

My mission is simple:

- I want writers to learn how to get ahead in this *business of show*, how to be smarter than their competitors, how to get noticed, how to develop relationships and, as rapidly as possible, begin to work with quality people and projects. If you do, you will build your resume and reputation as well as your success and satisfaction.

- I want you to make it on your own terms, not wait to be 'discovered' or rely on winning some form of cosmic lottery. To take that pro-active role, you need clarity and a plan, strategies that are simple and, when taken in combination, are the stuff of success in Hollywood. The tools, behaviors and ways of thinking that 97% don't know or won't do.

- I want to give you the tools to develop your career plan, and the know-how to execute that plan with clarity. When you combine your writing skills with a smart plan, you shift into a higher gear professionally. Use the strategies in this book as a starting point, power your plan with your own personality and style and goals in mind, act upon them as part of your daily routine, and you *will* create positive results.

If you believe you have the talent, then you deserve to do something real about it. In my view, you actually have an obligation, a responsibility, and a duty to yourself and to others to make your talent known, to do whatever it takes to share that talent with the world on the biggest stage possible.

Your reward will be your ROI, which no longer stands for 'return on investment' but for 'return on involvement'. What's required is the commitment to become deeply engaged, wholly and absolutely involved in your life and business, your dreams and actions, then to embrace those dreams and bring them into reality. That's the choice. That's the decision. If you decide, the steps are not that hard. But you need to make that choice, that commitment, or this book will be of no use to you.

If you choose to keep doing what you've always done, you'll keep getting the same results you've always gotten. But, if you're ready for a change… you've come to the right place! And once you've made that life-changing decision, continuous learning is the central key to your success.

STARTING TODAY

Since you're still with me, I take it that you're serious about making it in Hollywood as a writer. So it's imperative beginning now, beginning this very day, that you…

- Are focused, not random in your approach;
- Are clear, with an exact, specific and precise plan for success; don't allow any confusion;
- Learn what to do and how to do it, and recognize the missteps to avoid;
- Create rapport with the right people, and not waste time with the wrong people;
- Make real progress in your career by being a consistent and productive marketer.

I want you to learn what few know or practice, the things that allow you effortlessly and consistently to 'wow' people. If you follow the steps that I detail in this book, you will find yourself, on a daily basis:

- Knowing exactly what to do to rapidly shift your reality (in months not years);
- Taking small, defined steps every day, staying focused, and getting results faster than ever before;
- Actively managing your daily activities – and your attitude – with a sense of comfort;
- Setting detailed, achievable goals you can achieve now (not in some distant future).

As you start reaching those goals, you'll suddenly realize that you are:

- Overcoming fear of failure (risk may cause failure, but success cannot come without it);
- Blending your personality and easy professionalism in just the right measure (people don't know or care when you first meet if you're rich or poor, but they care a great deal how you conduct yourself);
- Regularly meeting new people with real capacity to influence (enhance) your career;
- Feeling suddenly more attractive to others (your confidence and authenticity will skyrocket);
- Consistently generating referrals and new connections (and accelerating your positive 'word of mouth').

Results start building until one day you realize that you are greeting each morning eagerly, excited to take the next step, preparing to win, and making small but meaningful daily deposits in your future success account. You will also recognize that you are:

- Smiling at the thrill of achievement (the shift from being fear-driven to success-driven becomes intoxicating);
- Less anxious and more patient because you're seeing actual results each week;
- Skillfully planning and managing the 'business' of your creative career, and clear about the difference between simply being 'busy' and making real progress);
- Having more fun (others will notice and they will ask what's changed);
- Bursting with energy, ready to drive right through the very middle of what most call 'impossible' to claim the success now within your reach – you've earned it, the right to be the person you are destined to be.

Once you reach that level of confidence and energy, you'll stop worrying about the 'competition', and stop taking advice from the so-called (wannabe) experts and instead focus on counsel from truly successful insiders – the very people you'll now know exactly how to target, access and develop personal rapport with directly. You'll be in the small minority that truly escape, once and for all, that cycle of doubt and drift and frustration. That little chorus of negative voices in your head will get thrown into the backseat, while you drive a sure and steady course to your desired destination.

Sounds good doesn't it? So how do we get there? Fortunately, there are only four pieces to your puzzle.

- **Passion**: knowing your 'why' (your *driver* – what drives you?).
- **Goals**: destinations broken down into specific, written action steps (in reverse order, from your desired destination backing out to wherever you are today).
- **Tools and strategies**: precise, reliable formulas for success to confidently guide your choices and actions for maximum result in the shortest amount of time.
- **Daily action**: without which, all inspirations, goals and dreams are mere fantasy. Awareness and knowledge are nothing without taking action! Action is the fuel that drives all success in life. Action on a daily basis. Action as habit.

It's Up to You.

Have you ever had times in your life when you kept hoping something would happen, that the answer you were seeking would come? Or, perhaps you kept hoping someone in your life would change so that your life would be better. How many times has hoping ever changed anything in your life? Never!

It is when you make a fist-pounding decision, and you say, "I will do it!", that something happens. The moment that you decide upon a matter, the whole universe goes into action to support you. The quality, the depth, the power of your decision is always honored.

You should decide upon a matter and it will happen!

~Jack Boland, The Secret Place

THE POWER, THE PASSION *PLUS*

The vast majority who pursue creative careers possess some degree of passion. That's also where most stop. Where most fail.

I assume you have talent. I assume you feel passionate about your writing. However, I don't assume you've been taught career literacy, business strategy, innovative marketing. Most don't talk about it or aren't willing to share their hard-earned trade secrets. That's why I've written this book. To lay out for you, in detail, how to create and translate your goals (with modest time investment by you) into very do-able action steps, based on proven strategies I've used to launch career after career. Just a bit each and every day. If your career truly means that much to you, this is a no-brainer.

One of the greatest truths ever uttered by Charlie 'Tremendous' Jones, the great motivational speaker and advocate for people improving their lives through reading, was this: "You are the same today as you'll be in five years, except for two things: the people you meet and the books you read." By far the more important is the people you meet. It's also been said you're the average of the five people closest to you, the ones you spend the most time with, and that's generally as true as it gets.

My life changed enormously only when I decided to up-level my relationships with mentors, and to befriend people far more successful than myself. That's the true alchemy of life. It's not mysterious, it's not difficult. It just requires seeing it for what it is, the truth.

However, it also requires a willingness to move out of the most uncomfortable zip code in this life or on this planet... your comfort zone. The very words *comfort zone* are a lie, a dangerous lie. It's the place where you settle, where you embrace your lesser self, smiling on the outside and riddled with insecurity and lack of fulfillment in your heart and your soul. Your soul's purpose fades from neglect. Many opt for this phantom *comfort* so they won't feel threatened, only to find – usually when it's too late - that was the single biggest mistake a person can make in this lifetime.

I say get the heck out of your comfort zone now, today, this second! Get on with your life, find your joy, be successful. Believe in yourself first, that's your birthright. Whatever you do, *don't be comfortable*. In fact, the more time you spend being uncomfortable, the faster you'll make progress.

If you know anything at all about yoga, you know it's about stretching. And each time you stretch, in fact, you grow yourself, literally. The next time you face that same challenge, that same stretch, it feels less. You become less fearful of attempting more difficult stretches. You become a better you. The only question is: when are you going to decide? When is now the best time for you to choose you?

One of the great outcomes you'll experience if you read this book and embrace my counsel, based on years of trial and error, is that you'll up-level your life. And you'll do it with precision, knowing what goals to set, the professionals to target (and why), knowing how to approach them (directly or via referral, a brilliant and simple strategy that simply acknowledges how well and predictably human nature responds to the right input). You'll master these simple ideas and more, and wonder what took you so long to truly, meaningfully *get in the game*.

You are absolutely capable of becoming part of the 'lucky' few who enjoy the creative and economic rewards of a successful screenwriting career.

Congratulations on your decision to take action.

Congratulations on caring enough about your career to do something about it and becoming the architect of your own luck!

Welcome to your future.

SUCCESS STRATEGY ONE: NETWORKING

The 30 Minute Short Cut to Your Future

The way of the world is meeting people through other people.

~ Robert Kerrigan

RELATIONSHIPS TRUMP RESULTS

The old adage goes *it's who you know* that gives you access and that speeds your path to success. The new adage is *it's who feels they know you*.

Building a supportive network is crucial in the development of your career. You must build your network strategically, applying criteria that serve your goals, and later in this chapter we'll be giving you specific strategies on how to do just that.

There's the *how* and the *why* of networking. First, the *why*. Recognize that a growing network with a purpose is a powerhouse. Network with individuals, join groups, and affiliate with those whose interests are consistent with your own. Do it intelligently – strategically – and without being too narrowly focused on a particular result.

As I mentioned when I referenced that quote from Charlie 'Tremendous' Jones ("You'll be the same person in five years as you are today, with two exceptions. The people you meet and the books you read."), the people you meet, the people you spend your time with, the people in your life are by far the biggest determinant of your life trajectory and of your success.

People tend to be a perfect average of the five people they routinely surround themselves with. Look around yourself. Who are the five people closest to you? Are they successful? Are they positive, healthy, optimistic and action-oriented people? Do they enjoy well-being, abundance and a sense of joy and reward in their business? In their relationships? How about an overview of their lives – spiritually, mentally, financially and physically?

My mantra and the key to all my success is simple: relationships over results, always. If you focus on results, frustration and disappointment will follow. Focus on relationships and better results automatically follow.

Networking is the single most powerful way to leverage yourself and your time, nurture new and existing relationships, and lay meaningful foundation for greater career success. And you can do the majority of it from the comfort of your home! In your pajamas.

Here's a fact: your network determines your success. Period. If you want to win in Hollywood, you don't wait to be 'discovered' in some random way. You develop relationships.

If you develop a clear idea of the kind of person you want to meet, the process becomes smarter and less time-consuming. If you have certain criteria in mind, you learn to network like a master without wasting prodigious amounts of time. Focus on the character, consciousness and capacity of people you want to draw into your inner circle.

Whatever and whomever you seek to attract into your life, be patient. Networking isn't all that different from hiring. Apply the same time-tested wisdom: 'Hire slow, fire fast.' Do your due diligence about people. Don't invest in people who are strictly takers, who don't have the same value system or positive beliefs or whose words and behaviors are either not in alignment or not 100% in sync with your values.

Success requires getting out into the world and showing up. It also requires you be selective and surround yourself with quality people (not just nice people, but *successful* people). So get out there virtually and, equally important, in the real world.

WHEREVER YOU ARE AND WHEN YOU LEAST EXPECT IT…

When I first moved to Los Angeles from San Francisco, I knew no one. For the first 12 months, I did one and only one thing: network. Before the Internet or Facebook had arrived, it was *mano-a-mano*, a day-by-day process of meeting, getting to know, following up with, getting referrals, sifting and sorting, until I found the caliber of people I wanted as the foundation of my life and Rolodex or address book.

How did I network so extensively pre-Internet? By going out of my way to meet and talk with people absolutely everywhere I went. The tennis courts and paddle tennis courts and swimming pool where I worked out every day was my 'base camp'. I started conversations at a local breakfast diner, at the coffee shop, at the local printer with whoever happened to be there, anyone walking around the townhouse complex where I first lived after moving to Los Angeles. In my eyes, wherever I happened to be was the perfect networking opportunity. Wearing a smile, I consistently introduced myself and asked questions of total strangers. This became my norm, my simple action-oriented philosophy. My goal was to discover a bit of information, a valuable idea, a lead or referral, ideally an ongoing friend and ally (like those I'll be summarizing for you later in Milestones). If I succeeded in even a small way every 10th or 20th conversation, I was a huge winner. I could easily meet ten or more people a day. If I won once a day, I could win 365 times in a year. That winning streak afforded me the knowledge, relationships and strong foundation to go on and create great success for myself in Hollywood.

And that's precisely what happened. I made quality friends and relations, and after that, it was just about showing up, working smart and hard, having taste and integrity, and staying the course.

FORGET POPULARITY, MAKE IT PERSONAL

Despite what you've heard in this age of social media, networking is not about collecting massive numbers of 'friends' or online acquaintances. Far from being a popularity contest, effective networking is seeking out and investing in *real* relationships with *quality* people.

People do business with people they know, like and trust. Networking is the fastest means to that end. Smart networking and social marketing strategies enable you to dramatically extend your reach and relationships quickly and with laser-like focus. Your mission is to develop enduring professional relationships, with the desired result of both real and virtual goodwill ambassadors spreading the gospel of you.

Done well, networking is the quickest and most effective way to create forward momentum for your career, rapidly connecting you to the very people you want in your inner circle. Intentionally target and nurture win-win relationships with people who have similar values, goals and the capacity to help and who, in turn, you can and will help in equal or greater measure.

Your targets are successful, professional contacts you may not have aspired to as yet, let alone had the opportunity to meet. Strategically planned networking is a dynamic tool with the capacity to catapult your career in unexpected ways.

INVEST MORE OF YOU, LESS OF YOUR TIME

If you commit to spend just 30 minutes each day networking (while using the other career-building strategies and tools in this book) you'll quickly feel more confident and in control of your career. You'll be able to measure your progress in months, not years. Feelings of frustration or helplessness will be replaced with the experience of success. You'll see small successes build into a larger successes.

If you focus on making just one new connection a day, five days a week, you will engage in a minimum of 250 new and relevant professional conversations in just one year. If you maintain regular contact with just 25-50 of them – that's just 10-20% of all conversations you initiate – you'll quickly build a formidable community, resource and foundation. Many of these professional relationships will naturally turn into friendships, and it's through these relationships and friendships that your Rolodex will explode exponentially.

Exercise this networking strategy for 30 or more minutes each day and you'll soon:

- Feel empowered because you're taking responsibility for your career's momentum;
- Grow in confidence because you've eliminated the uncertainty that plagues most creative people who relinquish control of their career path to others or to circumstance; and
- Mark substantial progress toward your personal and career goals.

Your upward success curve arcs up faster and faster the more connections you make with people. Your introductions, opportunities and relationships grow exponentially. As you increase the number of new people with whom you enjoy real rapport, they in turn introduce you to others, acting as both a quality filter and as your personal goodwill advocate.

And the three pillars of your career – your knowledge of the business, the opportunities opening to you, and the human capital available to you – will grow logarithmically as a result. When you're consistent and persistent, and make networking a natural part of your daily discipline, your return on investment – make that *return on involvement* – will make you rich with opportunities beyond anything you might have imagined.

NETWORKING AS A WAY OF LIFE... LIKE BREATHING

As a personal manager representing talent, I always felt 100% responsible for moving a client's career forward. Even if a client had an agent and/or attorney, I still felt 100% responsible. I expressed my enthusiasm by having a career plan for each individual client, and refining and taking action on it every single day. While every member of the team should feel that way, the person who should feel the strongest about that, of course, is you – the writer.

Agents and managers will play better tennis with and for you if you're making quality shots of your own. Nothing is as consciously and unconsciously motivating to a representative as a client who delivers quality information and contacts on a semi-regular basis. The talent who is active in the community, creating parallel and productive opportunities is a motivated and excellent client. That client is success in action and revenue will inevitably follow.

Just to be clear – and we'll be discussing representation shortly – networking is every bit as crucial *after* you've secured representation as it is before. Ask creative talent and the vast majority will swear they've gotten themselves more work or created more opportunity than their agent and/or manager. And it's usually true – it's just the way the world works.

People hire and work with others they know, like and trust. If people know, like and trust your representative, great. If people know, like and trust you, that's *huge*! The good news is you have absolute dominion over your future, your relationships, your progress and ultimate success.

IT ALL COMES BACK TO YOU

Every creative person should consider themselves primarily responsible for their career, for setting goals and taking daily action. If you've got an agent or manager, guide them but don't think of them as a substitute for you being out there networking and always extending your relationships and reach in the world. Representatives are not a shield to protect you or be solely responsible for marketing you. Continue to take responsibility for yourself and your career. Be the leader and the champion of your own creative career and that will inspire and motivate everyone around you.

Even when you have a team, the agent can make introductions, but you're the one who goes into the room and 'sells' yourself. It's a social business and we all find opportunity in direct proportion to the quality and number of our relationships.

PALM UP NETWORKING

When meeting new people for the first time, don't be in a rush. Don't make the mistake that 99% of all others make… immediately rushing in to ask their help, to ask a favor that's too big, too premature, too selfish, too early. Practice *palm-up* networking instead. That's when you enter into each new relationship with a metaphorical open hand; that signifies an attitude of giving, a spirit of service, and wanting nothing in return. Be curious and other-focused. Learn about the other person, develop rapport, be genuine, ask questions.

> ### KEY FOR WRITERS
>
> Unlike the actor, whose work and daily schedule are typically more social, your work is more solitary by its very nature. Nonetheless, commit to 30 minutes a day of networking. This practice will prove crucial for your success.

Always research or ask how you might contribute to the conversation or the meeting and add value for them. What are their professional and personal interests? What can you offer or volunteer in terms of your time, expertise, relationships to deliver value in return? Maybe it's simply the act of being genuinely interested in them, asking questions and truly listening to their responses (not thinking of what you'll say next, which is what almost everyone else does).

Focus and listen and you'll be handed clues and information and details that give you everything you need to develop and grow that conversation and relationship. If you're the exception to the rule, the one person that day who doesn't assault the producer, agent, or their assistant with your needs, asking favors before they even have a sense of who you are, *rapport* will subtly but quickly shift into *relationship*.

It's often the simple gesture that works magic. For example, if a new contact has impressed you, you can ask if it would be okay to write about them as a model of best practices when blogging or writing an article or contributing to a film industry discussion group online. Or simply volunteer to write them a recommendation on LinkedIn or for their website. These sorts of choices are thoughtful surprises, and tend to be greatly appreciated.

If you want someone to get interested in you, be genuinely interested in them. Without ulterior motive. Maintain an attitude of curiosity and openness and allow relationships to flourish. Perhaps engage them by asking the most valuable lesson(s) they've learned about film, Hollywood, networking, or whatever subject interests you most.

Better yet: Pretend you're not in Hollywood (literally or metaphorically). Pretend you're just meeting someone with whom you share common interests, and want to learn more. Ask smart questions, be gracious, let them know you value their time. On a call, let them know right up front you appreciate they're busy and only want a few minutes of their time; pick any modest amount. Be sure to offer to end the call no later than amount of time you requested. That's respectful and professional. If they extend the conversation, fantastic.

In a later chapter, we'll discuss the *Desired Outcome* strategy, which allows for a comfortable, smart, gracious and effective way to end the call and set up your next conversation.

THE 'WHO' OF SMART NETWORKING

Networking – both online and offline - has become an end unto itself, rather than a strategic means, for many people. Surprising numbers of people have become addicted to acquiring friends, creating the perception and reality of being busy, and confusing busy with business or being effective and productive. The time and effort devoted to acquiring and servicing (IM, text, email, Twitter, phone, etc..) those so-called relationships can exhaust you and others, without delivering any result whatsoever.

It's not so much how busy you are, but why you are busy.
The bee is praised; the mosquito is swatted.

~Catherine O'Hara

When it comes to networking, it's crucial to have a strategy. It's imperative to understand both *who* you wish to bring into your network, and *how* to effectively engage those people.

Always opt for the more personal form of communication to initiate a relationship. A handwritten letter makes a stronger statement than an email, phone is more personal than email, and a face-to-face encounter is always ideal. It may take time to arrive at an in-person meeting, but along the way be conscious of how you choose to communicate, all the while maintaining a warm, smart, professional demeanor.

And have fun.

Make people smile.

You'll be remembered.

Appreciate that every communication and interaction is an opportunity to be thoughtful and grow that relationship. Even if just confirming something via email, take the time to write something fun, unexpected, smart, helpful, informative, anything that will be appreciated, pique their interest, make you yet more memorable, and continue to grow your rapport.

YOUR TOP 100 LIST

If, over time, you could convince 100 people to champion you and your career, who would they be? Given your goals, your skill set and talent, the types of projects you think are right for you, who are the people across a variety of professional categories of life in Hollywood that would be valuable for you to know? What are the central things you want them to know and believe about you, so they'll feel motivated to help you?

Make a wish list of these people – the ones most important to your work, your goals, your life as you envision it. Put them in a spreadsheet.

If you can't access people on your top 100 list directly, who are their *influencers*? Who are the people surrounding them, within their company or inner circle, that they trust and collaborate with on an ongoing basis? Add those names to your spreadsheet. These influencers could be clients, employees, assistants, professional peers, colleagues, or friends.

I realize that you may not be able to start your list with 100 names. That's fine. Start where you are: maybe that's 25 names, maybe it's 10. Maybe fewer. But start – and build your way to 100.

Name	Title	Number	Address	Assistant	Assistant No.	Best Time	Recent News	Research	D.O.
Joe Mogul	Studio Exec	323-123-4567	2 Studio Lane, Culver City	Shara Future	323-123-4568 818-765-4321 (cell)	12:30-2:00 except Thurs	Got rights to new blockbuster novel	Yale grad Grew up in Boston	Personal contact before query
Randi Reader	Literary Coordinator	310-765-4321	3 Melrose, Hollywood	Bea Worker	same 310-555-1212 (cell)	Tue or Thurs morning	Moved from XX Agency	Attends Toronto Film Fest	Attorney to recommend?

Very importantly, if you were to speak directly with them, think through what the benefits and effects will be. What do you bring to the conversation? What precisely can they do to help you? What concrete thing would you ask of them to create a bond or rapport, and move you closer to achieving your goals? Be sure you have a column for this important element.

Your target list should embrace a small number of quality names across the many different job descriptions in Hollywood. Your list might include a number of producers, directors, agents, managers, executives, acting coaches, casting directors, even cinematographers and editors and others. While agents and producers are approached constantly, there are others (like cinematographers) who rarely get approached but who may be more available and reachable. Indeed, they may not only be happy to share their wisdom and counsel, they may be able to refer you to or introduce you to others who could be important to your career. Not every aspiring writer – maybe not even 1 in 10 – will think to approach a cinematographer, or an editor, or a line producer. To be strategic, you need to think differently.

Of course, you'll research what you need to know about the people on your target list. Beyond the obvious and endless source of information you have at your fingertips via Google, you can find countless websites and references to research credits, film and TV projects and people, including their history or bios. Between Google, press clippings, blogs, articles, and free websites, you've instant access to a treasure trove of information. For individuals, of course, you'll also want to do a quick search on Facebook or LinkedIn, just to find whatever additional or personal information or history may be available.

ONE BECOMES TWO, THEN THREE, THEN...

Not in the first call, but as people come to know you over time, they'll often either volunteer names of people they think you might want to meet, or respond to your questions by suggesting specific people. For example, you might ask their opinion about the one, two or three smart young representatives they most respect. You're not asking them to go out of their way and make a direct introduction, but you can then call one of the names mentioned and reference the person who was saying such positive things about them. It's a door opener and conversation warmer. Very effective. These kinds of relationship-expanding opportunities will become your common reward if you are diligent and committed to persistent, consistent networking.

You might ask which projects they've most enjoyed working on recently, and then go one level deeper by asking about particular people they've worked with (again, producer, casting director, etc..).

If you succeed in creating meaningful rapport and having ongoing conversation with just one person in each category, you will have been the architect of a huge win for your career.

By developing your personalized target list for networking, you will be creating your *magnetic north*, the direction in which your internal career gyroscope always points, keeping you focused, networking productively and for maximum benefit.

You will continuously add to and refine your list over time. Working on your list or spreadsheet is a perfect way to jumpstart your day, giving you the confidence of knowing exactly what you need to do that day, who you want to initiate contact with in the 30 minutes you've allocated that particular day. Even if you haven't identified by name all the folks you want on your Top 100 list, you'll have parameters, categories or titles that will sharpen your networking. You become systemized in your marketing. It becomes stress-free and manageable. You instantly avoid all the confusion or randomness that plagues your competition.

A well-maintained spreadsheet is worth gold – it's your career's *Information Central*. You don't want to rely on your memory to keep track of who you've spoken with or left a message for, on what date(s), what was discussed, what you learned about that person, when you'll be in touch again (your *follow-up*), the names of anyone in the office you've met (e.g. the assistants we'll be discussing shortly), projects or clients you've learned they're involved with, what if any materials you submitted, ideas for your next call and so on.

The result? You're prepared, you're thorough, you're in control, you're ready to move on to your next call.

Surround yourself with people who believe you can.

~ Dan Zadra

SOCIAL MARKETING AND COMMUNITIES

In today's online world, social communities provide an extraordinary opportunity as well to connect quickly and efficiently with quality people you may want to know.

Networking online is not much different from the chamber of commerce, a college alumni association, church or neighborhood. Yet, the advantages of online social communities and the opportunities to market yourself are so vast and efficient, they dwarf the old-school alternatives. You can be in hundreds of places at once, speak with or ask questions to hundreds of thousands if not millions simultaneously, perform a detailed search of many millions of people. Your audience is self-selected, available, accessible and open to professional interactions.

Leveraging social communities can be a valuable tool, but only if done with laser-like focus. Don't allow your online experience to consume too much of your precious time. For too many, social communities become a wormhole, an addiction devouring hour after hour, all productive focus flying out the window, with questionable result at best.

The key is to be selective and not waste time. I recommend setting a strict time limit, spending no more than 15 minutes a day researching and using

> ### A QUICK CAVEAT
>
> Be cautious about joining any organization or group, web-based or otherwise, that charges a membership fee, promising access to Hollywood connections. Generally, these will be non-productive and are frowned on by those within the film and TV communities who are genuinely interested in connecting with new talent.

social platforms. You're looking to achieve a maximum result in minimum time. Be sure to follow up and follow through with the people you do choose to meet online, the same way you would for people you meet via phone or in person.

Remember, the intention of all this networking is the same — you are:

- *targeting* the contacts you want to make,
- *filtering* those contacts through your interaction with them, and then
- *migrating* them to the next level.

So someone you connect with via Facebook moves up to an email relationship; which develops into a telephone relationship, and that yields a meeting.

If you deem someone important enough to connect with online, commit to developing and sustaining rapport, even if simply via email. More often than not, the old-fashioned and more personal approach of phoning people inevitably works better, wastes less time, and gets better results.

YOUR ONLINE PROFILE: A 21ST CENTURY BUSINESS CARD

If you choose to network online, write a complete, compelling, high-impact and concise profile. Your profile page within each community acts as your personal web page, on-line resume and marketing face to the world. These sites are the business cards of the 21st century.

Your profile page may very well be seen by thousands of people. Make it distinctive, honest, a statement of your passion and history, goals and purpose. Authenticity and transparency are key. Be genuine and articulate clearly who you are, your work and passion, your experience, whatever distinguishes you, what you're looking for, and how people can get in touch with you, including the web address of your website or blog you want people to see.

To optimize your profile, carefully choose language that includes what you do, what you want, and employs good use of the keywords that describe you professionally. The content of your profile is picked up by the search engines, including every photo and video, keyword and phrase. Thus, your social community web page will turn up in results from web searches by all web users, not only those within that particular social community. Always include a clear photo of yourself, which makes you friendlier to other users.

WHEREVER YOU ARE

Opportunities for networking are all around you, closer than you think. And the good news is that you don't have to be in Los Angeles to start. Here are some of the options that are waiting just outside your door:

CHARITIES AND ORGANIZATIONS If you're inclined, join organizations as an extension of your own networking. Do it if you believe in the cause and the value of contributing your time. Go on a

Habitat for Humanity build or volunteer to answer phones during a PBS pledge or join the Special Olympics, and you may find yourself rubbing shoulders (or sharing phone lines) with a variety of entertainment industry professionals. The organizations mentioned are not suggestions, nor are they necessarily the likeliest place to make connections, but they're all doing good work nonetheless.

FILM FESTIVALS AND BEYOND There are a vast number of film festivals, geographically dispersed all over the U.S. and elsewhere. There is likely a film festival near you and it might be well worth attending. Some are stronger magnets than others for certain categories of industry professionals, including film distributors and agents (e.g. Sundance, Tribeca, Toronto, Telluride), but all draw heavily from the creative communities of writers, directors, producers and a host of other independent film professionals. Assume most people you meet in the film business are eager to find a great new talent. Circulate, be yourself and meet as many people as you can.

ALUMNI ASSOCIATIONS AND CHAMBERS OF COMMERCE The American film industry imports people. The vast majority of successful people in the film industry hail from somewhere other than Los Angeles. Wherever you live, there are no doubt success stories at the mid and upper echelons of the film and TV businesses who came to Los Angeles from your hometown or home state, or who attended the same college or university as you.

When researching online, use search criteria to identify writers, directors, producers, studio executives, or any others who are from your hometown or who attended the same school as you.

College or university film and theater departments and chambers of commerce traditionally track alumni or locals who've created a successful career in Hollywood. This sort of information and shared background can give you a psychological advantage and a friendly bridge to reach out and create new relationships in Hollywood.

FILM COMMISSIONS Every state has a film office or commission, sometimes housed within another state office, such as a Department of Commerce. Most major metropolitan areas have their own film office as well. These are easy to identify by simply searching state or metropolitan government websites. Phone your local film commission to learn if any professional organizations in your area host events or mixers for their creative communities; if not, suggest they do so and jump in to help organize such an event.

The vast majority of these offices also publish annual directories, as do local Chambers of Commerce. If not, an in-person visit will work miracles and you'll walk away with a lot of information. These directories are treasure troves of information, listing every film-related person, company and resource within their jurisdiction. Pay attention also to the advertisements, especially those highlighting organizations and festivals.

From these film commission directories alone, you can contact other creative professionals, learn about groups or organizations, and identify categories of resources within the commission's area including, among others:

- talent agencies and management companies
- production companies
- producers
- directors of photography
- editors
- production designers
- location managers
- unions, guilds and associations in the local area.

Networking is part science, part art, part magic and never a linear or predictable experience. The only reliable truth is you will grow a valuable Rolodex if you are consistent and imaginative.

At the end of each chapter, I'll be giving you a quick summary of the points we've covered. I'm calling these *Milestones*, and this definition seems particularly apt for our purposes here:

Milestones are constructed to provide reference points along the road. They can be used to reassure travelers that the proper path is being followed, and to indicate either distance travelled or the remaining distance to a destination.

MILESTONES

- RELATIONSHIPS TRUMP RESULTS. Remember that people do business with people they know, like and trust. Concentrate on building relationships strategically so that you form a strong foundation for an enduring career. Good relationships lead to positive results.
- PALM UP NETWORKING Approach each new contact with an open, giving hand. Be curious, ask questions and stay other-focused so that you add value to the relationship.
- YOUR *TOP 100* LIST Create a spreadsheet with your own personalized target list of the 100 (or 25, or 12) people you most want to connect with; including a variety of job descriptions across the Hollywood landscape. Don't forget assistants!
- SOCIAL COMMUNITIES Join and create profiles within online communities, using keywords that insure your profile will be picked up by the various search engines. Find the people in film and TV who have the biggest online followings; ask questions of them, let others see you interacting with them. Beware, though – social media can turn into a wormhole. Don't let it occupy more than 15 minutes a day
- ATTEND FILM FESTIVALS AND CHECK OUT LOCAL FILM COMMISSIONS Film festivals are an excellent way to meet agents, distributors, filmmakers, producers, actors, and other writers. Volunteering is a great foot in the door. Your local or state film commission probably has a directory with information about professional film industry-related organizations in your area. Join, attend, and volunteer to help create events, mixers, etc.

So now that you're starting to build your network of relationships, just exactly what is it that you'll be telling them about? You'll be telling them the story of you – brand YOU – and that's what we'll be covering in the next chapter.

SUCCESS STRATEGY TWO: BRANDING

The Haiku of *You*

Always be a first-rate version of yourself, instead of a second-rate version of somebody else.

~ Judy Garland

Every successful business has a brand statement. World-class copywriters, ad agencies and branding experts get paid huge fees to study, research and refine a company's message to effectively communicate the brand value of their enterprise.

I'D LIKE TO BUY THE WORLD A COKE...

So what really is this 'brand' that people pay huge sums to discover, create, refine? How do you begin to define your brand and why should you bother? Where does branding end, and marketing begin?

Coke's 'brand' is celebrated as the most globally-recognized, effective, well-known brand in the world... period. It's a red can with the product name boldly written in a distinctive, instantly-recognizable cursive font. It's that way in China, in Argentina, in Norway and North America. The product inside that ubiquitous can, the soft drink whose secret ingredient remains a mystery, will taste identical wherever you are.

The experience externally (as a brand) and internally (the experience or taste as you drink the product) is reliably consistent wherever you happen to be in the world.

The Coke 'brand' is universally known, however, not because the brand is so clear and consistent. It's because Coke has consistently, persistently and brilliantly *marketed* their brand in every conceivable medium year in and year out for decades.

Marketing comes in many sizes and shapes, from TV to radio, outdoor (billboards) to print advertising to direct mail, from radio to the ever-expanding realm of digital (online) opportunities. Coke has been relentlessly activist, spent billions on building and supporting their brand, and continues to market 24 hours a day, 7 days a week, all over the world. That's fierce marketing. That's what it takes to best your competition, to achieve and maintain the biggest market share worldwide, to thrive as a brand and as a business, targeting every living person on the planet.

A brand, very simply, is how we, the public, identify with a company or its product. When we think of Nike, we think of *Just Do It*. It's not the product per se, but what we think of or how we relate to the product. What does Nike want us to 'feel', what kind of impression does Nike want to create in the marketplace?

THE NIKE IN YOU

The same is true for you. Thankfully, however, you don't need to market to the entire world. You don't need to spend billions of dollars. Your market focus is much more precise, so you don't need to spend hundreds of thousands for an ad agency to create your brand, or millions more to produce commercials, buy media and advertise your brand.

But you do need to be able to answer—for yourself and for others—the following questions:

- Who are you?
- Do you have a 'vein of gold' as a storyteller?
- What distinguishes your craft and talent?

BREAKING THROUGH THE CLUTTER

Our society celebrates the exceptionally gifted: architect or attorney, banker or baker, chef or chauffeur, designer or deejay. But if no one is aware of their talent and uniqueness, the baker and chef have no customers, the architect and attorney have no clients, and nobody has any business.

Once you identify your brand and are able to articulate it confidently and succinctly, it's time to crank up your marketing efforts and make a bigger noise. Maybe you're the writer-equivalent of a red can with silver cursive writing, or a different kind of experience that comes in different packaging (glass, aluminum, plastic), maybe your most amazing, natural gift is for live stage, or half-hour comedy, or writing a great villain for a feature film or hour TV drama. You cannot market yourself effectively until you truly, down in your bones, *Know Thy Brand*!

The clearer and more specific your brand — as evidenced by the way you talk about yourself, communicate your talent and goals to producers, directors and beyond, the way you 'walk into the room' — the easier you make it for others to see you in the correct way and to hire you. And that means you will establish more quickly your foundation for greater success.

> Example: **Nora Ephron** was the acknowledged queen of the rom-com. Did you know that early in her career, she wrote a regular column for Esquire magazine on women's issues? Her first major screen success was *Silkwood*, which made it clear she could write strong roles for women. Then she began her string of successes with *When Harry Met Sally*, *Sleepless in Seattle*, and *You've Got Mail*. Her brand, which she recognized early, and then made deeper and wider, was writing about and for women.

> Example: **Quentin Tarantino**'s reputation is rooted in his capacity to make extreme violence entertaining– from *Reservoir Dogs*, to *Pulp Fiction*, to the various installments of *Kill Bill*, to *Django Unchained*. And only he could extend his brand into comedy with the still violent but funny *Inglourious Basterds*. Try to imagine another filmmaker pitching that one.

> Example: **Trey Parker and Matt Stone** are best known for their many seasons of *South Park*. But they also extended their brand from half-hour TV animation to feature film animation with *Team America*. And, in a giant leap, they recently triumphed on Broadway with their award-winning *The Book of Mormon*, but in each case they have their brand of smart, irreverent comedy.

THE BIG *IF*

You want to be brilliant, you want to succeed in the midst of the dogfight of competition that is the reality of film and TV writing, and you can do just that... IF!

If you invest the time, if you get feedback, and if you learn exactly and precisely how to define and communicate your brand in a single phrase, you're halfway to your goal.

Of course, you'll commit to taking action every single day to market yourself, to create new opportunities by networking and initiating new relationships, and to spread the gospel of your brand.

You'll research, read, ask questions, get feedback, go with your heart and gut and, once clear about your brand, you'll consistently infuse that into the DNA of your entire marketing toolkit. Every time you reach out to someone new, or people you've met but haven't seen for several months, you'll use these same marketing materials to follow up on your conversations and meetings. You'll refresh their memory, keep yourself top of mind, reinforce your brand.

We're going to talk about the nuts and bolts, the basics you'll return to and use again and again and again. So it makes sense to invest the time and thought that insures they're the best they can be, reflecting brilliantly on you and serving you well.

THE WRITER'S MARKETING TOOLKIT

Whether you're a writer, producer, writer-director or any other type of 'hyphenate', your marketing toolkit is key to taking control, taking action and building your success in Hollywood. It's what separates you from the other 97% who lack these tools and haven't been taught what they are, why they're so essential, and how to create and use them successfully.

What's inside your marketing toolkit and why are these tools so essential?

- Logline
- Query Letter
- Pitch and Advocacy (your "other" pitch)
- Leave Behind
- Testing and re-testing of all of the above, including your screenplay itself

- Table readings
- Your *Top 100* List: systemized research and outreach which we covered in the chapter on networking

Your personality, energy, ability to engage people, along with the above building blocks, are the tools that will attract people to you and your projects. Where the actor's marketing toolkit might include a headshot, reel and monologues, the writer or producer's toolkit will look more like the above list, possibly including a budget and/or executive summary for a given project. Everyone should also seriously consider producing or being involved in a short film to showcase your talent, and you can refer to that chapter in this book.

It would be impossible to over-estimate the true value of your pitch or logline or other marketing materials. We want to warm up our audience (executives, filmmakers, financiers, agents, etc.) before we simply thrust a feature length script (or book or other property) into their hands.

Agents are busy, producers and managers are stressed, executives and directors are overworked. Supply exceeds demand, and no one can read every script or take every meeting offered to her or him.

You have one chance to make a first impression, to capture someone's attention, to get your metaphoric and literal foot in the quality doors of Hollywood. Since you want to hear "you had me at hello", it's worth investing a significant number of hours over the coming month or two to 'nail it', to make your presence and presentation undeniable and irresistible.

Your marketing toolkit deserves as much if not more attention than the last screenplay you wrote or produced. Why? It's your calling card to the world, your opportunity to create a positive, memorable first impression, and increase your odds of being asked to submit your materials and come in for a meeting. Most pay scant attention, invest far too little effort, thinking a matter-of-fact query will suffice. The typical logline or query or pitch or other marketing tool is ineffective, too lengthy, and thus rarely successful in capturing people's attention in a meaningful, measurable way.

If your goal is to make yourself so attractive that people feel no choice but to read more or get on a phone call or meet in person, invest every ounce of time, creativitoverovery, thoughtfulness and intelligence you can muster. Communicate *you*, not just your project, in a way that forces people to want to know more. More about you, more about your story.

Whatever time you invest toward your desired outcome will repay you in ways you cannot imagine. People will share and pass around your material if it immediately captivates them.

Whether your goal is to…

- Sell a 'spec' script
- Option your most recent completed screenplay
- Land a writing assignment and get hired
- Persuade investors to finance your new 'indie' film project
- Attract the agent or manager of your dreams
- Get a 'name' producer to take a meeting with you
- Attach an actress or actor to your project
- Find the perfect director for your script
- Get a director or producer interested in you for his or her upcoming project (e.g. to rewrite it or polish it)
- Attract distributors, sales agents or producers reps to your project
- Or rapidly expand your network of people who think you're talented, personable and someone they should be paying attention to and 'talking about' to others

…it all comes down to the same thing: becoming an ever-smarter marketer and learning the tools to communicate powerfully *why you* and *why your project*. It's a highly competitive business and to make yourself stand out from the crowd, to get your scripts read, gather a quality team, and get in the room, there are some non-negotiables you must master.

Get committed to focusing on more predictable, measurable, step-by-step career growth; to being a brilliant advocate and marketer, rather than suffering the frustration and uncertainty that plagues most who adopt a more passive approach.

When you approach your professional life as if you were an entrepreneur in any other business, you will recognize the similarities. After all, you are:

- Creating a product (we'll use your screenplay as the model here)
- Protecting that product (copyrighting your script and registering it with the WGA)
- Writing supporting marketing copy (your logline, treatment and synopsis)
- Practicing your elevator pitch (no different than your pitch in film or TV)

- Identifying your list of targets or customers (your strategically researched and targeted Top 100 List that builds your team and network of successful allies)
- And crafting a compelling marketing letter (your query letter).

Admittedly, the marketplace is competitive. The good news is that success in Hollywood is a bit counterintuitive.

The business is engaged in a perpetual search for that fresh new 'voice', that talent that they can claim to have 'discovered'. And that kind of success you create each and every day as you move forward. It's not a resume or history we use as a soapbox. A good history, of course, is a bonus, but for most of us that takes some years and several projects. Meanwhile, the film and TV communities are constantly finding and recruiting new talent (even if you have to pay some dues, including lower pay initially and no statuettes on your mantle). The bottom line is you can create a professional network that points to an enduring and successful career long before you have even one film in theatres or one series on television.

THE REWARDS OF PERSISTENT, SMART MARKETING

Pretty Woman was originally written as a drama, an indie film, that I got accepted into the Production Lab at Sundance. That was my dream Desired Outcome. The lab gets far less global recognition and publicity than the film festival, but Hollywood pays close attention. Being one of a couple of handful of screenplays in that year's program, the writer and I returned from Utah to find ourselves invited into countless meetings about that project and beyond. One marketing strategy unleashed a tsunami of quality opportunities and set the writer's career on a very exciting trajectory. Meetings and/or projects with James Cameron, Oliver Stone, Dick Donner, Joel Silver and many others followed. We produced that film under the Disney (Touchstone) banner, and *Pretty Woman* played in theatres non-stop for 6 continuous months. That was just part of my reward for consistent, persistent marketing.

Albeit subjective, talent is a bit more of a meritocracy. A majority can usually agree on the merits of a screenplay, a TV show, a performance. But marketing is not a meritocracy, and the main reason is because so very few creative talents ever engage or learn to become self-responsible for the marketing of their own talent. For the few that do, suddenly it's less about the competition and more a focused campaign to build strong bridges with quality people. And that progress is measurable and real. And it pays huge dividends. And it shaves years off the success curve for the truly committed creative person.

Success is a choice. It's preparation, discipline, having a marketing plan and executing that plan little by little, day by day, without second-guessing your results for the first 6 months. And, of course, applying the same discipline to your craft (it's a two-sided coin that wins the day, talent and marketing). One without the other is a daydream.

No experience often trumps experience. You've never had a development deal that fell flat. You've never had a film that didn't open successfully. You're the new yet-to-be discovered voice that will excite. So it's important to set the stage to be 'discovered', because creating that opportunity to become an 'overnight success' takes time!

SO WHAT'S IN YOUR MARKETING TOOLBOX?

LOGLINE

Whether yours is a film, TV series, stage play or other creative project, your logline is your project's brand statement. One sentence, possibly two, that sum up absolutely the core of your project.

Loglines: History, Purpose and Value

The logline was born during the early studio days of Hollywood. Each studio archived countless screenplays in their vaults. Stacks upon stacks of scripts. It became their habit to have a story editor or reader write a concise one-line summary of that script's story on the cover and often on the spine of the script itself. This allowed directors, producers, executives and actors to scan huge stacks of scripts to search for a project – a love story or horror film, an action film or comedy or drama – without having to un-stack all those screenplays.

Today, a compelling logline is powerful because it's often employed not only to initially attract a producer or agent or director (which it is), but also because it can be useful throughout the life of a project in a variety of ways that might surprise you. It's a one-sentence summary that can be readily communicated – verbally or in correspondence – not only by you, but from assistant to executive, from producer to director, from agent to actor. It's a powerful tool you'll incorporate when applying to screenwriting contests or to attract representation. Very importantly, if your logline grabs people's interest right away, it will often be adopted by the very story analysts at the studios and other major companies (including the larger agencies and management firms) whose responsibility it is to write 'coverage' on your screenplay. Simply put, it will be 'codified', attached to your script, and seen by the very people on whom you want to make a favorable impression - agents, producers, executives, financiers and the like.

Quality Counts

A well-written logline is an art and discipline that can increase response rate for your queries 25-50% or more. A logline that piques people's interest will distinguish you and make your letter stand out, and make your phone conversations more engaging. Used at the beginning of a verbal pitch, it will immediately orient and engross your audience, setting a powerful context for all that follows.

Some writers would prefer not to be responsible for marketing their work in general, including the challenge of distilling all their hard work into one or two sentences. But it's imperative and, done well, a game changer.

Some are purists and believe people should want to read their screenplay in its entirety because, after all, it's amazing and the only real way to assess their craft as a writer. Unfortunately, that's not the reality of the business of film or TV. In a world of hyper-busy producers, agents and executives, with so many writers and screenplays being circulated, a truly stand-out logline will cut through the noise.

Put yourself in the shoes of a producer who is looking for a brilliant story from a writer who cares enough, is so professional, such a good 'partner', that they've taken the time to craft a world-class, bullet-proof, tested and re-tested logline that the producer in turn can use with confidence with financiers, studios executives, sales agents, talent managers and beyond. You've just made their job dramatically easier and made you and your project far more attractive. Very motivating. Your attraction quotient just hit the top of the charts.

If you're super well connected to top name talent and producers and studios and financiers (*and if you are, thanks for reading this book!*), then maybe it's not necessary. Unless that's true, however, it applies 100% of the time to 100% of your work. If you want to gain the attention of people who matter in Hollywood, if you want your scripts read, then commit to exercising the same care, devoting significant time, writing and rewriting repeatedly your logline.

But Wait, There's More…

A great logline also often survives to be deployed across editorial (reviews and journalism) as an advertising tagline, for TV listings, in press releases and EPKs (electronic press kits), among other uses.

A great logline minimizes the risk others will come up with their own bad or lesser version of a description for your project and use that when communicating with talent or their boss or other decision makers.

This varied and well-travelled and potentially long life is the very reason your logline deserves significant time and attention, rewriting and testing. To make sure it drives people to want to read your screenplay or script.

Beyond that, it's your 'voice'. It's not a factual summary or academic treatment. It's usually the first exposure (or the first in a long while) to your writing for the majority of your audience of Hollywood decision makers. It's a first opportunity to make a splash, to be memorable, to indelibly surprise and leave your reader with a sense of your 'voice', of your profound gift as a writer they should then feel eager to read and meet.

Your logline should spur people's imagination to see the movie poster, the DVD cover, the film itself. It should inflame their imagination and curiosity about the lead characters (highly cast-able, of course), and deliver a palpable sense of tension. The overall storyline should scream 'audience pleaser' and – oh yes – be highly marketable.

A compelling, undeniable logline will also become an anchor for your pitch, and much like pitching, creating a near-perfect logline for your story is not a natural skill set. It's a talent that, like screenwriting itself, must be learned, practiced and refined. If it takes writing a dozen or more loglines, picking the best of and rewriting those 3 times each week for a month, do it. Begin while still writing your screenplay.

Better yet, some writers form the habit of creating the perfect logline before they ever sit down to write the actual script. It becomes their north star. I highly recommend you do this as well.

Either way, it's non-negotiable. Crafting a riveting, effective logline for your screenplay is your responsibility. It's critical if you want to stand out and have agents and producers reading your material. No one else will do it, no one else cares as much as you, and without it, you're at such a huge disadvantage it will be ten times harder to market or pitch your project. Phone calls, in-person pitches, query letters, every attempt to market your project relies on a logline that shines, that effervesces with the excitement of your unique story, that makes your story stand out from the competition.

THE ELEMENTS OF A LOGLINE

After a twister transports a lonely Kansas farm girl to a magical land, she sets out on a dangerous journey to find a wizard with the power to send her home.

You know exactly what classic film this logline refers to, don't you? In fact, even now, some 60+ years since that film was released, the logline alone can summon up images in your mind.

Loglines are to screenplays as haiku is to epic poetry, serving to convey the dramatic story of your script in the most abbreviated manner possible.

No character intricacies. No subplots. One sentence. Two sentences only if your script and story are exceedingly complicated. Most writers will assure their story is special, complex and complicated and thus justifies a two-sentence logline. Let's safely assume that's not true. One sentence will do, assuming you can divorce yourself long enough to think like a marketer rather than a writer. Don't bond to all elements of your story. Get to the center quickly.

There are 3 basic elements or components to a logline.

- **Who the story is about**
- **What the character strives for**
- **What stands in the way**

Who the story about

Unless your story is about a truly famous person, never use the character's actual name. Employ descriptive words and phrases, remembering that each word must be chosen for ultimate effect, communicating heart, emotion, humor, tension and the like with the absolute fewest words possible. As an example, *who* might best be described by the character's occupation or a well-chosen adjective. In the rare instance where the protagonist is actually an ensemble or group, it's best to select a single word such as *crew* or *survivors*.

In *The Wizard of Oz*, rather than mention the central character's name (*Dorothy*), the more visually and emotionally descriptive phrase is "a lonely Kansas farm girl".

What the character strives for

Again, in *The Wizard of Oz*, avoiding all plot intricacies and other characters (no Tin Man, no Lion, no Scarecrow), this lonely Kansas farm girl merely "sets out on a journey to find a wizard with the power to send her home".

What stands in the way?

The epic approach would include mention of the Wicked Witch and the perils faced by Dorothy, but the haiku approach might simply be "she sets out on a *dangerous* journey".

So we've eliminated the yellow brick road, the villain, her cohorts, and avoided getting too wed to the story's elements, opting in favor of communicating in short, simple fashion just the heart of the narrative. Where Dorothy has multiple goals along her story's path, her ultimate goal is to return home.

The logline quoted earlier, originally written by Brian A. Klems for *The Wizard of Oz*, conveys beautifully the heart of this classic story:

After a twister transports a lonely Kansas farm girl to a magical land, she sets out on a dangerous journey to find a wizard with the power to send her home.

In one sentence, it establishes what's at stake, that something will be lost if she doesn't succeed (some form of risk or death or loss, literal or figurative), and yet we leave the audience wondering how the story ends. By answering those three simple questions, and choosing carefully the words or adjectives that flavor your story, you've the ability to communicate in one or two sentences a great deal about your characters, the nature of the conflict, the distinctive tone of your story, the setting and central action of the film.

OTHER KEY CONSIDERATIONS FOR YOUR LOGLINE:

Always keep the protagonist at the forefront of the logline. This encourages directors, producers, financiers etc. to visualize a 'castable' leading role or star vehicle.

Always opt for active or external choice of verbs and words in general. We often see loglines using words like: learns, realizes, chooses, decides, finds, etc. Wherever possible, substitute words that express tension and action, words that are visual by nature, such as *struggles* or *escapes* or *uncovers* or *flees* or *fights*.

Since we want to think of our protagonist as a leading actor of the day, that character must be active (not reactive) and initiate or turn the story forward in a decisive way. So even if he or she is essentially reacting to events, choose active language that makes it seem they take action in a way that causes events to unfold. A good example of this would be where our hero is on the run from the law, as in the case of *The Fugitive* (e.g. A doctor, falsely accused of murdering his wife, struggles on the lam as he desperately searches for the killer with a relentless federal agent hot on his trail.).

That's another key rule for loglines: a good logline boasts a story that is <u>not</u> dependent on its ending. And it's always best not to suggest how it ends, not because it saves space (which it does), but because it leaves people curious, wanting to learn more.

And that's the three-part formula in action: *who* the story is about, *what* the lead character strives for, and *what obstacle* stands in his or her way. It communicates the essence or spine of your story, the sentence your entire story hangs on, and serves to excite the imagination and attract people to the possibility of a great and satisfying 'read'.

By the way, you can use 'sci-fi' or 'action' or 'comedy' or other attribution if it helps clarify your logline, but the genre or tone is often best communicated by your description itself.

GET IN THE HABIT

Read, review, study, search out as many loglines as possible. Scour TV Guide, IMDB.com, newspapers, reviews in newspapers and online, The Hollywood Reporter, etc.

Practice writing loglines for recent films you've seen or classic films you know well, or as an exercise each time you read another writer's screenplay.

WHICH WOULD YOU WANT TO READ?

Here are a few more examples of loglines that demonstrate varying degrees of intrigue for the underlying story. See which ones would make you want to read the screenplay.

SPEED: A cop must save a busload of innocent people imprisoned on a bus that will explode if it drops below 55 miles per hour.

RAIDERS OF THE LOST ARK: An archeologist is hired by the U.S. government to find the Ark of the Covenant before the Nazis.

LIAR LIAR: When his son wishes he will only tell the truth, an attorney who's a pathological liar is magically compelled to be honest for one day and struggles to win the biggest case of his career... without telling a lie.

MINORITY REPORT: In a future where criminals are arrested before the crime occurs, a despondent cop struggles on the lam to prove his innocence for a murder he has not yet committed.

Write loglines for each of your projects. Plan to write and rewrite your own loglines even more than you rewrite your scripts. A good exercise and practice is to spend 10-15 minutes each day rewriting your logline.

Don't try to perfect it all in one sitting. Write it and set it aside, review and revise the following day.

Repeat that over the course of a couple of weeks, possibly with more than one version of your logline. Let it marinate and percolate, get feedback. Keep looking at your logline from different angles, using different words and phrasing, changing around the order in which your one or two sentence logline introduces the basic elements, the placement of your adjectives, the overall energy of your logline. Go back, look at it, try crossing out any individual words that don't elevate your description of your film's main elements, tone or the heart of the piece.

As with anything you write, your logline will reflect your voice, talent and professionalism. No different than a synopsis, query letter or your screenplay itself, it's imperative you never send out a logline or other writing with even a single 'typo'. Grammatical errors, misspellings or the like will instantly flip the switch on a reader's enthusiasm. It's both a conscious and subconscious response. So just make certain your work is clean, clean, clean before ever sending it out.

THE QUERY LETTER

Pat, a screenwriter, once sent me the following question:

"If you don't have a cousin's next door neighbor's pool man's godchild that used to date a guy that met a producer one time at a bar and you have no previous professional writing experience and you have not won a major screenwriting contest, how do you get people to at least accept a query letter?"

Be Different

The vast majority of people send out queries, period. Perhaps they wrote and rewrote those letters until they were the very best letters imaginable. Often not. Yet, almost none have researched their intended target or recipient, let alone their company, let alone their assistant. They haven't been taught to. They weren't taught to think creatively about their career, to have the confidence to color outside the lines, do it their own way and not the standard, impersonal way.

Even more rare is the creative person who, having done their research and discovered connective tissue, actually had the presence to pick up the phone, call the assistant to the person they were targeting, introduce him or herself, immediately begin building rapport and a bridge that can grow stronger with each interaction. Before they hit the 'send' button or mail the envelope. Maybe 1-3% think to introduce themselves as a human being, act curious about the people they would address a letter to, bother to make the other aware of your existence and of your project, but rather just mail an envelope from a complete stranger that arrives as a surprise.

The more personal and direct your contact and communication, the better your results. Experiment by phoning the assistant before you send query letters. (In the next chapter we'll go through the steps of making the arrival of your query letter an *expected* event. In doing so, you'll gift yourself the advantage of naturally following your submission with an expected, pre-arranged follow-up call.)

Of the queries I receive, 99% arrive unexpected and 'unannounced.' The vast majority give no indication they've researched either me or my company, let alone why their project might intrigue me or be a good match for my company. You can put yourself in the top 1%. Pick up the phone, call the assistant, introduce yourself and your project and make your query a friendly and expected event. What's the worst that can happen? What if only half are available for a brief phone chat and invite you to forward your query letter? You've identified in advance those who are more welcoming, more willing to look at your materials. Then you can actually track your progress. How many calls you placed, how many query letters you actually mailed or emailed, how many gave you their direct email address, how many actually read and responded to your query. Collecting this information is worth gold. It transforms your marketing from a random series of events to a systemized business.

These precious moments spent in a phone conversation introducing yourself to new people on the inside of the business not only allow you to interact before submitting your work or query letter, they also offer the perfect opportunity to ask questions, flatter people by seeking their counsel and receiving answers that teach you valuable information. (In my experience, these conversations also put you in the top 1%, making sure you stand out from your competitors.) The more you do it, the more comfortable it becomes, the more you'll be motivated to step up your game. Developing the habit of live interaction can lead to a virtually endless Mobius of human opportunity. And it doesn't matter where you live. Anyone can begin practicing this strategy today.

Today, it takes only several minutes to learn everything there is to learn about someone from the internet. Just Google people and find where they went to school, companies they've worked for in the past, articles or announcements in the trade papers about clients or projects they've been involved with, charities and hobbies and other interests. Look on Facebook, search IMDbPro.com, or pay $12.00 a month to look folks up on *whorepresents.com* to see all of an agent or manager's clientele.

Because you never know what one piece of information you'll unearth that will make "the" difference. One of the screenwriters in my mastermind wrote me the following email:

> *"I was able to get a producer's assistant to accept a logline and synopsis via email. The producer has a lot of credits, including winning an Oscar (for privacy, I've deleted the name). The producer and I both attended the University of Virginia, and his assistant accepted my email based on that connection. I also learned that the producer is from Virginia and recently produced a script by a Virginia-based writer."*

That to me sums up the value of investing a very small amount of time for a potentially giant return on your investment of time. An Oscar-winning producer agreed to look at materials simply because the writer took the time to do a bit of research, pick up the phone, ask a few basic questions and was rewarded with that one nugget of information that created a very warm welcome.

Of course, the quality of your work matters, whether it's a logline, synopsis, script, query letter, or a short film. People are judging the quality of your writing, down to the formatting and syntax and spelling. Same with visual materials. So please treat your query with the same care you would bring to your logline, your screenplay or anything else you send out into the world. It's your signature and voice and face to the world and you want it to reflect you in your very best light.

Don't limit yourself to who you *think* would be open to receiving your query. Don't pre-judge or assume people don't want to review your work. On the other hand, don't paper the town, but be persistent in reaching out to those who you've researched and put on your Top 100 list because they are aligned with your talent and goals and current project.

Even if a company doesn't generally accept screenplays other than through an agent or other representative, you can still submit your query, you can still develop rapport with the assistants. The goal should be building rapport with valuable, well-placed people, not necessarily optioning or selling your first, second or third screenplay. If they review your query and won't accept your script without a release, sign the release. If you can't get someone on the phone, don't be discouraged. Send your query letter. If there's no response, calendar to send it again in 3 months' time. Stop with that particular query and that particular office only if and when you receive a verbal or written rejection or 'pass'. If you submit a query and get no response over the next 60-90 days, feel free to re-submit your query to a different individual at that company. It may be something as simple as the person you'd addressed your letter to has moved from that company.

DOS AND DON'TS FOR YOUR QUERY LETTER

The do's…

- Include the title of your screenplay in the reference line at the beginning of your letter.
- Your logline should appear no later than the first sentence of the second paragraph, preferably in your very first paragraph. Depending on your style, you can even open the letter with your logline.
- Follow with a brief well-written synopsis (maximum 6 sentences). Don't attempt to convey the whole of your story; leave them wanting more and asking for your script.
- Find your own style, but whether in the third brief paragraph or otherwise, be certain to include some personal or biographical information. Although less is more, making it personal, even with a single line why this story is so compelling and relevant to you as a writer, can only help. Make each line count, so the reader sees your natural gift as a writer.
- Rewrite your query, dozens of times if need be, until it 'sings'. Get feedback and make certain it's ready for prime time before sending it out. Remember, the recipient will be judging your writing craft.
- Don't inundate your reader with too much information, which may unintentionally provide opportunity or reason for an objection.
- Celebrate the opportunity to make a brilliant first impression, and be certain to include all appropriate contact information (but don't go overboard and include links to your social media profiles or other extraneous information).
- Craft your prose so that it's crisp and articulate; grammar and spelling count, as does accuracy and neatness (be sure both your letter and the envelope are typed, not handwritten).

- Your entire query letter, including salutation and close, must fit comfortably on one typed page, and not look crowded.
- Address your letter to a specific individual, never to a company, address them by name and thank them for their time at the end of your letter.
- Proofread your letter: no typos, use proper syntax, and please confirm you've spelled each person's name correctly (it's worth a quick peek at the Hollywood Creative Directory or a quick phone call to the assistant).

Have fun! Make your letter truly reflect who you are as a person and as a talent; come across as a mature, confident, talented, calm and easy-going individual (i.e. one who would be fun to work and spend time with.)

Some don'ts: what to avoid in a query letter...

There's legitimate opportunity for a difference of opinion, but I discourage query letters that boast loglines and synopses for multiple projects at the same time. I've received letters that run 2 to 6 pages, describing 3 to 15 projects, which I always ignore. It's not my job to review a shopping list of a writer's entire inventory, let alone decide which may be the best work or the project which is most recent and thus the freshest. Yes, I learn the writer is prolific, but it also makes me curious about their history and why so many projects are being 'shopped'. I prefer a writer who turns my head about one amazing story and communicates why it's so special. The bucket approach diminishes any sense of excitement.

Here are some examples of worst practices:

- Being long-winded or overly verbose, which is just bad writing and shows lack of clarity;
- Silly, self-effacing, cute or obsequious language (if using humor, test it on 10 people to see if it truly gets a smile or laugh);
- Gimmicks: don't send a package with a 'prop' or gift or other items;
- Name-dropping (unless it's a legitimate referral);
- Bragging about a good coverage from one of the major agencies; *(Note: the larger agencies often protect themselves in the event a project gets greenlit by having on hand a 'positive' coverage to*

give their star clients; however, they won't give it to them before your project is set up at a studio, and since these coverages are never made publicly available, it's not credible that you would have seen such a document.)

IDEAS YOU MUST AVOID IN YOUR QUERY LETTER

- Suggestions that so-and-so is currently reading your script, which almost always feel designed to create a false sense of urgency, unless corroborated by an attached letter evidencing same (e.g. letter of intent signed by an actor or director).
- Claiming anything which is not true or cannot be supported with documentation, e.g. 'I have partial financing' or 'actor X wants to play the lead role', etc.
- Supplemental material, DVD, tagline, casting suggestions, marketing concepts, etc.
- Using pre-addressed mass mailing labels; these can be purchased at bookstores or online, but scream 'impersonal' and often contain misspellings or out-of-date addresses.
- Simultaneously querying two or more people at the same company at the same time. If the company is small, it will be obvious and will likely annoy; if the company is large, all incoming scripts are 'logged' and 'covered', so once again they'll know and it will likely not be a welcome practice.

- Hyperbole: do not praise your own work or suggest it will make $100M at the box office; do not reference praise by others, which can often backfire or just seem too 'sales-y')
- Immodesty or overselling of any kind; avoid subjective words like 'unique', 'commercial', 'blockbuster', 'amazing' or any other value-laden adjective.

NOTE: As discussed earlier, it's perfectly acceptable to query multiple different production companies at the same time. Just avoid whitewashing the town, and limit your submissions to a small number of companies (perhaps no more than 3) until you've had sufficient feedback. Once you get consistently positive feedback, you can expand your outreach, so long as you're not submitting to 15 companies at the same time. It is a close-knit community. More importantly, you want each submission to truly target your top choices.

- Never call an office or send a query letter about your project unless that screenplay or material is 100% ready to be sent. If a producer or agent or representative should request your script, it's imperative you deliver it expeditiously. Do not make the mistake of getting a 'yes', then not send your script because you begin to second-guess yourself and launch into a 3-week rewrite. Do not squander opportunity or relationships in that way.

AND finally...
Never send a screenplay or other material without permission.

PITCH

Great stories deserve a great pitch, and you deserve to receive the disproportionate benefits that are the direct and often immediate result of delivering a great pitch.

The 'pitch' has become a time-honored, institutionalized part of the process of setting up any film or TV project in today's Hollywood. Pitches are an everyday reality in and beyond Hollywood. Pitches are how we communicate most effectively and economically about the two most valuable currencies in all the film and TV business: brilliantly inspired fresh projects and the talent that birthed them into the world. Both currencies – you, the creative talent, and the new project you're pitching – are equally valuable.

We'll go into extensive detail on your Pitch in a later chapter, as well as the Leave Behind. And before we wrap, we'll also discuss Testing and Re-Testing all your tools (including your script itself), and the often-ignored but powerful tool of Table Readings.

COVER LETTERS AND CORRESPONDENCE

Many of the elements we covered above regarding query letters apply to all your correspondence. Any and all letters should be brief, never more than one page including address, salutation and your information and signature at the bottom. Every letter should be simple and concise, effectively communicating exactly what you're looking for – e.g. 'this is who I am' (i.e. your strengths) and 'this is what I seek' (e.g. type of representation).

Every office receives hundreds of cover letters, if not more, each month. The long cover letter tends to go unread. The short, clean cover letter tends to get read. The sloppy cover letter with misspellings or poor grammar, or the letter that does not immediately, succinctly and clearly state its purpose, may likely end up in the trash.

Take care when writing any letter, whether a physical letter or an email. (Too often, people treat email as a lesser form of communication, a 'quick' note that merits less time and thought. Wrong!) You are judged by every action you take, by every communication regardless of form. Treat every opportunity as important and deserving of your full attention. If it's worth sending, then write it and set it aside, review and revise it before hitting 'send'. Make certain it reflects well on you and communicates with clarity, class and personality. Disclaimers at the bottom of an email (e.g. 'Sent from my Blackberry or iPhone, not proofed for accuracy') signal laziness and should never be used in a professional context. It may be okay to use with Aunt Jennie, but not when addressing anyone important to your career (and that includes assistants).

The key to success is *brevity*. Crisp, clear, clean communications that can be consumed in a glance will deliver better results. If it can be read while 'on hold' or walking down the hall, it's more likely they'll read it and hand it off to an assistant for a response. So it's best to avoid unnecessarily long messages. Similarly, unless it's a personalized 'thank you' note, it's generally best not to send handwritten communications.

MILESTONES

- Know your brand, who you are, how you and your talent are perceived, and what is your 'vein of gold' as a storyteller.
- Develop your toolkit: Craft your loglines, polish your queries. Each one is an opportunity to get your foot in the door.
- Make every email and letter count. Take the time to communicate crisply and professionally, and edit every communication so it's clear, free of ambiguity, misspellings, and as brief and to-the-point as possible.

Okay, now we've covered that network of relationships you're developing, and clarified your focus on the brand you're building, what's next? A strategy that will separate you from 95% of your competition: with every call you make, every meeting you take, you'll be focused on what we're calling your D. O. List.

SUCCESS STRATEGY THREE: YOUR D.O. LIST

What to Say, How to Say It, and When!

The victory of success is half won when one gains the habit of setting goals and achieving them. Even the most tedious chore will become endurable as you parade through each day convinced that every task, no matter how menial or boring, brings you closer to fulfilling your dreams.

~ Og Mandino, Author

Here's your next new rule: starting today, right now, you will never dial the phone, you will never leave home without knowing your D.O. list and what your follow-up will be.

What's the deal with the D. O.? It's your Desired Outcome...maybe a referral, maybe an appointment, maybe an actual assignment. That's the short term outlook. In the longer term, it's the human communication equivalent of looking at a map (like those big maps you see in a mall) and seeing a big red dot labeled 'you are here' and tracing with your finger the shortest route to your destination.

Make a conscious point to use this simple strategy in your next several conversations, and you'll be amazed. When you see how powerful and how quickly this one strategy speeds up your progress, you'll feel as if you traded in your tricycle for a Ferrari. It will quickly become your habit from this day forward, without even giving it so much as a moment's thought, to incorporate this strategy reflexively every time you reach out to someone. This one mindset and strategy wipes out the uncertainly and confusion that plagues almost everyone climbing the

Hollywood ladder, and gets you where you want to go far more quickly and efficiently, shaving years off your success timeline.

By weaving your desired outcome and your follow-up into conversations right up front, you come across as professional, you enhance the likelihood of good results from every call and every meeting, and you greatly increase your opportunity for continued dialogue and rapport-building.

How big a relief would it be to know you can stay in control, communicate calmly and with confidence, all the while you're guiding or empowering others to help you get exactly where you want to go? Without vagueness, confusion, uncertainty. Huge relief, yes?

So exactly what is your D. O.? How do you effortlessly frame your desired outcome, while embedding your follow-up plan into each conversation at the same time?

Imagine you're on the phone to someone who could be very important to you. You want to build a relationship with them, you want them to get to know you and your talent. It doesn't matter if you're talking to an assistant or directly to a producer, a manager or a casting director. You have in mind one single outcome, the one specific result you want from this conversation. It's not a menu or multiple of outcomes. One result only, a very precise and easily communicated action step and result. And you know precisely what it is before you ever pick up the phone.

Examples could include: you want to send your query or your script, you might be seeking counsel, or asking for a recommendation (e.g. agent, manager, etc..), you might be introducing them to someone and adding value for them, or it could be you want to set a meeting. You're focused on just one singular, specific goal for that phone call or meeting.

DON'T RUSH IN

Don't dive in headlong with your question or request. It's certainly not the first thing you utter when on the phone or when you walk into the room, maybe not even the second thing. Wait toward the end of the call or meeting, or at least until you've enjoyed a couple of minutes of conversation and some rapport has been established.

Crisply, succinctly framing your desired outcome is your way of mapping the coordinates for what will happen next, your way of guiding the actions and expectations of the other person, before you end the call or leave the room.

Be aware that the majority of people go into a call without knowing where it will go, without having a rock solid goal; as a result, they are vague or exploratory in their approach, which often leads to a stumbling, awkward communication.

But you, with your D. O. list, communicate with clarity and confidence. That naturally makes the person on the other end of the phone feel more comfortable and more likely to say 'yes' when you comfortably describe a precise, easily achieved outcome. You make it easy for the other person to deliver without investing undue time and effort.

KEEP IT SIMPLE

During your first call with someone, the desired outcome must be something quite small and manageable. Your goal is to make it easy for them to say 'yes' to you, to establish a momentum that can be built on.

In that first call, target a desired outcome that requires little effort and time on the assistant's or other person's part. Make it easy. It is to your benefit at this stage to focus on rapport and relationship, and setting up the opportunity for a second and third call. The majority of people ask big favors on the very first call, requiring too much on the part of a virtual stranger. You, however, see the opportunity to be innovative and different. You see the opportunity to begin a new relationship, to begin a friendly dialogue and not rush into making big requests.

A VIRTUAL GRAB BAG OF CHOICES

Here's a handful of examples of manageable, clear calls to action:

- Ask for one piece of specific advice (a question you have prepared in advance);
- Ask for a referral to or, better yet, their opinion about an attorney they regard highly;
- Ask the names of one or more younger literary managers they think are smart and effective;
- Get their permission to email them your writing samples;
- Ask if it would be okay for you to quote them or write a positive blog entry about them (using their name as a role model); or
- Offer to make an introduction. Explain that you've heard many compliments about them, and would love to meet eventually, but

in the meantime can you make a potentially valuable introduction to them (e.g. the smart development executive, script consultant, agent or producer you've just met).

Your D. O. list is limited only by your imagination. Your goal is to initiate ongoing conversation and rapport-building opportunities and, with each interaction, to increase momentum, professional intimacy, and trust. So be creative and, for each call or interaction, come up with a simple desired outcome that makes it as easy as possible for the other person, no matter how busy they may be, to say 'yes' to you.

RINSE AND REPEAT... intelligently, intentionally, in intervals

Intentionally 'stage out' your requests. It not only makes it easier for the other person to say 'yes', but also hands you the perfect opportunity to have continued, ongoing contact and conversation. Regular rapport-building contact is the far bigger 'win'. You're building your network, and, as we covered in our first chapter, networking is the single most important factor in leveraging your time and your talent, and in creating a strong foundation for your career.

Ask too much right away and you diminish the likelihood of multiple interactions. Ongoing conversations are the difference between a one-time request and building a real relationship which, in the long run, is the far greater value. Go for the big 'win' by intentionally asking little, designing the opportunity to keep in touch, and truly getting to know the other person.

APPLY STRATEGY GENEROUSLY... no matter who your audience

Often you'll be speaking with a person's assistant. (We'll be discussing the world of Assistants in the next chapter, but the art of dealing with assistants and your desired outcome is just that...an art.) In that instance, subtly but consciously transition that person from being someone's assistant to being the 'boss'. You do this by being friendly, showing respect, asking questions, not attempting to rush past them to their boss, by choosing empowering language and, importantly, by addressing your request to them personally. Shift the dynamics. Give them a promotion by addressing them 'as if' they are the boss, seeking their counsel and advice. Most people treat assistants like rugs, but not you!

The process of 'building' relationships in Hollywood often begins most effectively from the bottom up, not top down.

On the other hand, if your call happens to be answered by their boss, go for it. Whoever answers your call, you're prepared and ready. You have your desired outcome worded in your mind, ready to slip into the conversation when you feel the time is right – no matter who answers the call.

SUCCESS IS IN THE FOLLOW-UP

This is where 97% of people lose their way.

Have you ever had people express interest in you, ask you to submit your materials, only to wait and wait, but you don't hear back? Now what? What do you do? Do you pester them? And if so, by email or phone? How long do you wait?

Most people aren't comfortable when it comes to follow-up, but it's one of the most critical elements of relationship-building, and of success in every area of life. Done properly, it's natural and comfortable. Done wrong, it's a source of awkwardness and frustration.

Follow-up serves you in three major ways:

- First, you stay in control, you manage others' expectations, you know with confidence when to call, you don't allow a submission or conversation to drift or become neglected, you stay out of confusion and awkwardness;
- Second, you naturally create the opportunity to learn if the person has done what you asked, not being in any sense disappointed if they've not yet; and
- Third, whether they have or not, follow-up is your free pass to increase the frequency of your conversations, create more intimacy, build more foundation and relationship. Follow-up is your all-access backstage pass, your golden opportunity to continue to build every new relationship. In Hollywood and in life, relationship is the most valuable currency of all, so effective follow-up becomes mission critical if you're serious about succeeding.

It's easy and should be a natural part of every single conversation, never a source of uncertainty or anxiety. Just remember to set up the expectation of follow-up during your very first conversation. Let them know they'll be hearing from you. Not sometime soon, but at a very specific time, e.g. 'a week from next Tuesday at 1 pm'.

Just like your desired outcome, you plan your follow-up before you ever dial the phone. It's only a sentence or two, but a critical piece of your result and relationship strategies. If you didn't have a goal in mind, you probably wouldn't have picked up the phone to call that person. So it follows that follow-up is an essential ingredient for every business call you ever make. The same holds true for every in-person meeting.

When you call to follow up and speak to that person's assistant, you may learn their boss is not available or hasn't yet gotten to your request yet. Just be ready and say 'no problem, I'll get in touch again in 10 days, or on such and such date'. Your tone remains confident and relaxed and in control. There's no sense of confrontation or disappointment. You simply agree to call back (again, for example, 'next Wednesday at 10 am'), and put that on your calendar.

This sets a balanced tone, making your communications professional yet personal.

This is second nature for me and occurs every single time I make a professional phone call, regardless if to a stranger or someone I've known for years – or their assistant. Whether an hour, a day, a week or two, even a month, I always set an expectation when that person will hear from me again.

NO MATTER WHO ANSWERS THE PHONE, IT'S THE PERFECT PERSON

Remember, your desired outcome is your secondary objective. Your primary goal is growing new relationships.

So don't be in a rush to end phone calls. Any call may present the perfect opportunity to chat for a couple more minutes. Have in mind some other 'conversation' or a question, some way to engage the person on the other end of the phone and learn something new, something more that allows you to continue to add dimension to that conversation and relationship. This is a key part of your follow-up practice and strategy.

Always be prepared and take advantage of every opportunity to advance your rapport one step further. Consider the assistant and his or her boss as one and the same person. They enjoy an extremely close working relationship, and the more the assistant likes you, the better off you are. They talk to each other all day long, every day, and a positive comment about you from the assistant will absolutely help shape the boss' opinion or sense of you.

You can accomplish the same thing in a cover letter by choosing any one of an endless set of possible minor requests. For example, you could suggest 'The thing that would help me the most and provide the greatest value is to receive your candid feedback about my logline. At the close of your letter, simply mention that you'll phone (e.g. 'a week from today') to allow them ample time to review your materials. You come across as clear and respectful and professional, effectively managing their expectation about your interaction.

You've just gifted yourself a wonderful opportunity to talk again.

EVERY CONVERSATION EQUALS OPPORTUNITY

My motto is: never ever let an opportunity pass. Even rejections are opportunities. View every person, meeting and interaction as a vehicle to legitimately establish and grow rapport. Even if the response is not initially favorable.

Remember how we started Chapter One: *Relationships trump results.* It's keenly important you always move your relationships forward. Remain positive, remain focused on your goal, be vigilant while appearing outwardly calm and personable.

Confidently and casually establish not only the expectation of follow-up, but place the ball squarely in your court, letting them know right up front that you'll be the one who will make contact. This is a key part of the strategy. It takes the onus off them, one less thing for them to remember and do. You gladly accept the responsibility – and the advantage – of being the one to initiate each next communication. The bonus or benefit is that you keep control of the conversation, all the while appearing considerate and professional. Your follow-up then becomes an expected event — and you don't risk being perceived as a stalker!

If setting a meeting is part of your follow-up plan, you have your calendar out and ask them to pull up their calendar. It's all very comfortable, very matter of fact.

You'll ask their 'best email' to send whatever they may need to review. Never ask permission, assume it. Confirm their direct phone number. Again, don't ask permission, simply ask 'what is your direct line at the office?' Never ask 'can I have your direct phone number?'. The latter approach invites a 'yes' or 'no'. The former inevitably insures they simply give you the information you desire.

Take the pressure off both of you by letting them know upfront you're cool yet professional. Let them know it's not essential they've done as you asked by that date, but you'll check in with them by a specific date regardless.

I leave them with just enough time to make my request reasonable, yet brief enough that the frequency of our conversations begins to create a subtle sense of momentum and familiarity.

Building rapport with someone new should be a relaxed and very intentional process, the cumulative result of repeat conversations. It's precisely the type of behavior an agent and/or manager would engage in on your behalf when introducing you to a broader spectrum of folks in Hollywood.

THE RULE OF 3

The Rule of Three is a well-known concept in both writing and oratory dating back to classic times. Think Caesar's *Veni. Vidi. Vinci.*

Jump ahead nineteen centuries or so to Lincoln's famous line in the Gettysburg address: *a government of the people, by the people, for the people.*

In fact, I first learned of this rule when I was in law school and was taught the primary lesson of communicating your message to a jury: *first, tell 'em what you're going to tell them; next, tell 'em; and third, tell 'em what you've told them.*

There is a certain magic to this Rule of 3, some kind of internal geometry that gets to the way our minds work, and that's an important rule to know in building your network and your brand.

The first time you call, the first time you introduce yourself and your materials, you are 'new', a stranger, someone they're learning about for the first time. You are expressing your desire to make yourself known.

The second conversation or mailing is different. You're somewhat familiar, but not yet a known commodity. But with your call or mailing, you are emphasizing – underlining, if you will – the fact that you are a professional, committed to working toward your future.

By the third time, however, you are more familiar, more of a regular presence. You are now *memorable.*

And so it is that after three exposures, three repetitions, people naturally feel more comfortable with you and pay better attention. In turn, you're more comfortable communicating with them. The rule of three: it's just the way our brains are wired.

A DAILY EXERCISE

If you incorporate the D. O. list and the follow-up habit into your schedule and do this on a regular basis, initiating even just one new call per day, your comfort level will increase exponentially and quickly. Imagine initiating five new contacts each week, the majority leading to multiple conversations. Each month you'd be reaching out to twenty new people, following up and enjoying a second and third call, growing your Rolodex far beyond what most consider possible or realistic. But it's entirely realistic and do-able without stress, with an investment of very little time on your part. (By the way, you're not excused from this daily exercise even if you have a day job. Figure out how best to fit this into your schedule.)

The benefit doesn't stop there. If only half of those newly-developed relationships yield one referral over the course of the coming year, you'll have exploded your Hollywood connections by well over three hundred new friends in the coming twelve months. That alone spells success.

Even when – after following the guidelines of our upcoming chapter - you've assembled your dream team of agent, possibly manager and attorney as well, you'll still make use of these strategies on a consistent basis. The most valuable connections or relationships are the ones you build yourself. Remember, 'it's not business, it's personal.'

MILESTONES

- For each call or meeting, know your desired outcome and your follow-up BEFORE you make the call or walk through the door.
- Increase your opportunity for success by having one request and result clearly in mind, something that makes it easy for the other person to say 'yes'.
- Be specific, but be patient. Don't lead with your request at the very beginning of a phone call or meeting. Even if it's only a minute, let the conversation warm up.
- Keep your requests very simple when initiating a new relationship; your goal is to have a follow-up plan for that simple desired outcome that allows you to comfortably stay in touch and keep the conversation going.
- Use your new D.O list and follow-up strategies with absolutely everyone, whether a top casting director or a producer's assistant.
- Never leave a conversation without first creating your next opportunity to speak. Set a task, along with a specific day and time you'll get back in touch, and immediately enter it on your calendar.
- Never ask permission but confidently and casually ask their 'best email and direct phone number'.

We're well along the road now: you're networking each day, still honing your brand, and mastering your D. O. list. Now, who are the first people you'll make an effort to reach out to? The most important people in Hollywood, that's who: The Assistants.

SUCCESS STRATEGY FOUR: THE ASSISTANT...
YOUR MOST VALUABLE ASSET

How To Access, Empower and Befriend The Gatekeepers

Always be nice to assistants.
They are the real gatekeepers in the world.

~ Anthony J. D'Angelo, author and motivational speaker

The most important people in the film and TV business, by far, are the assistants. Revere them. Befriend them. Treat them with unadulterated respect. Know their names and make them your allies.

There's a vast and easily identified sea of people - all critical and connected, available and ambitious - that you can tap into directly, instantly gaining enormous advantage. You can easily contact and invite into a conversation any of the many hundreds of assistants throughout Hollywood. The same is true for all the younger executives who've graduated from their assistant jobs. They're all quite accessible and capable of being your best allies and strategic career partners. These are your prime collaborators and co-conspirators. They are your fast track to measurable forward progress and career momentum in Hollywood. They go by a variety of different titles...

- Assistant
- Director of Creative Affairs
- Creative Executive
- Director of Development
- Manager of Production

Every one of these titles describes someone who's been vetted and is now on the 'inside', performing essential entry level work for agents, managers, casting directors, producers, studio executives and more. They log an extraordinary number of hours each and every week, rarely enjoying a day off, in their quest to move up the ladder, create relationships, and learn how the business works from the inside.

Bear in mind that being an assistant is never their end goal. It's a highly sought-after and competitive perch which, once achieved, is their golden ticket, since it provides them unparalleled access to information and a broad spectrum of people across the Hollywood landscape. And your goal is simply to be strategic, befriend them in a professional context, make them your goodwill ambassadors and thus act as your bridge to the people that matter in the film and TV worlds of Hollywood.

CREATIVE EXECUTIVE PAVES THE WAY TO STEVEN SPIELBERG

Over the course of numerous phone conversations and several face-to-face meetings, I'd built rapport with Mitch and he had become a friend. At the time, he was a creative executive at Amblin (pre-DreamWorks), reporting to Steven Spielberg. I sent him a beautifully-written screenplay, knowing it was anything but a blockbuster. It was a 'small' story, an intimate piece about adolescent characters – not typical fare for Amblin, let alone for Mr. Spielberg. Mitch read the script and phoned to say he enjoyed the story, but that it would be a 'pass' for Amblin.

I asked if he felt the script was well-written, if it was poignant, despite being a small film, the kind of story most would describe as 'indie' fare. He said 'yes'. I then asked if, based on the quality of the material, he'd have any cause for embarrassment giving it to Mr. Spielberg to read personally. He said 'no'. I urged him, as a personal favor to me, to have this most revered creative filmmaker read what might well be a 'pass'.

And he did. He put it in Steven Spielberg's 'weekend read' stack of scripts. The following week I got word he'd loved the script and wanted to buy it. Within a matter of days, both Warner Bros. and Universal Pictures made competing offers on Mr. Spielberg's behalf.

None of this would have been possible had I not invested in getting to know Mitch, creating a comfortable rapport based on trusting and liking one another. Mitch was not president, let alone a senior executive, at Amblin. But he was a trusted 'creative exec'. It's never about going to the top, but about going out of your way to create rapport with people who are 'on the inside'. Our relationship was the only reason Mitch gave this unlikely script to the biggest director and producer in the film business.

I've built my successes largely thanks to the bridges I've built with assistants and other 'entry level' but highly motivated and smart people who in turn are trusted by the producers, directors, casting directors, studio executives, agents or managers for whom they work so hard. And since human nature is constant and predictable, I cannot overemphasize the effectiveness and importance to your career of embracing this 'gatekeeper' strategy.

CREATING AN ALLY

Whether your ultimate goal is to make yourself known to a producer, director, casting director, agent, manager, studio or independent film executive, treat their assistant with respect and courtesy, humor and politeness. Do not 'rush' your way through the assistant or approach them as someone standing between you and your goal.

While some perceive assistants as walls or limitations, you know better, and your attitude is exactly the opposite.

Approach the assistant as if he or she is precisely your desired objective. Communicate your appreciation without being overly solicitous. Use your precious moments on the phone well, stating clearly who you are, your purpose and your 'why'. Your 'why' is about the assistant, the regard you have for their company, and your mission or goal that prompted your phone call.

In advance of your call, research as best you can the assistant, the assistant's employer (both their boss and anything you can learn about their company), and the films or TV shows they or their clients have recently been associated with. Include in your research hometowns, schools attended, interests and charities, and any other information you can learn. (You might want to check back on Chapter One and the researching tips there.)

Know as much as possible about the person and company you're calling. That few minutes of research you put in can make a huge difference, providing grist for valuable and far more comfortable conversation. In addition to building your confidence, it will also distinguish you from your competition, demonstrate your professionalism, and provide 'common ground' between you and the person on the other end of the phone.

If you don't know the assistant's name in advance, ask that right up front and then research them again after your first phone call. A quick search on Google will likely yield a treasure-trove of insights and information.

TIME IS PRECIOUS

The assistant is working in excess of 12 hours each day. They're reading scripts, juggling phones, doing errands, arranging schedules, listening in on meetings, taking calls on the weekend, and often feeling beleaguered, ignored and undervalued. They pay extreme dues and bear an extraordinary workload.

In addition to performing every task imaginable - e-mails, faxes, filing, scheduling, running for coffee or ordering flowers - assistants generally answer over 100 phone calls a day. Do not attempt a lengthy chat or you'll find them putting you on hold and becoming anxious. Make the most of your initial 30-60 seconds to ask their name, be friendly and courteous, and make them smile. Ask one simple, useful question and thank them properly.

Some assistants are more approachable, and others will be too harried or act self-important, or merely be having a bad day. If you run into that, quickly assess if you can be the person who changes their day for the better with empathy, humor and/or thoughtful conversation. If not, simply and politely suggest you'll call back at a better time. Or seek out a different person at that same company. Find your next new friend and court them to create an ally.

A NETWORK THAT GROWS TOGETHER

Much like you, the assistant is eager to matriculate and move up the ladder of success. They have larger goals and ambitions. Their stifling work schedule includes access to decision makers and a super-insider education about the tools of the trade. Thus, they're in prime position to grow their title, influence and income. And to help you do the same!

They are your peer, colleague, and co-conspirator in the making. Never forget this is the one person who has constant and primary access to the agent (or producer, casting director, director, executive). The assistant is the gatekeeper to the very person you want to learn about you and your work!

The assistant has a keen grasp for the tastes of their employer, and they'll be far likelier to champion your work – or at a minimum, pass it along – if you've included them in this way. If an assistant likes and hands your screenplay to their boss, that person <u>will</u> look at your materials.

Address your question or needs to the assistant. Empower them, make them important. Seek their opinion, assistance, answers, knowledge. Do not attempt to leapfrog over them to a 'more important person' at the company. Direct yourself to the assistant, not their boss, and you will be the extremely rare person approaching them in this way. If you consistently apply this strategy with assistants, you will:

- Stand out in their mind (and Rolodex);
- Receive a quicker response;
- Develop greater personal rapport while creating reason for further communication;
- Benefit from having the assistant personally review your materials (creating a bond and empowering them); and
- Get the assistant 'invested' in you, greatly increasing the likelihood they will ask their boss to review your materials.

MAKE IT PERSONAL

Always begin an initial phone conversation with a simple yet powerful question: ask their name. From that call forward, always begin each successive conversation by greeting them – by name! This may seem common sense and simple, yet I promise it has a magical effect.

You'd be shocked to learn how anonymous assistants feel and how few people take the time to properly greet them, let alone by name. I often sense a tone of surprise when I greet the assistant by name. I can actually sense their shoulders relax, hear the change in their voice. The assistant manages an endless series of urgent calls that begin with 'so and so calling for so and so, is she (or he) available?'. The tone is often rushed, sometimes simply rude and dismissive.

But you're going to be the exception!

Introduce yourself properly, and always ask if they are busy and if this is a good time to speak. If it is, introduce yourself, ask your question, seek their advice and be concise yet relaxed. If it's not a good time, simply offer to call back at a better time. It's the little things that will set you apart and make you 'user friendly'.

Unless you truly need to speak with their boss, plan to conduct initial business with and through the assistant. It saves time, gets messages and documents safely to their destination, all the while adding dimension to your relationship with the assistant. It pays dividends.

The assistant who feels her or himself to be on the receiving end of a consistently enjoyable and substantive rapport and conversation will go well out of their way for you. The assistant who feels treated as an 'equal' can and often will work miracles -- procuring home numbers, making certain your materials are at the top of the stack, contacting people while on holiday, or satisfying any of a myriad of possible needs.

EFFECTIVE COMMUNICATION

In your initial call, volunteer to email the assistant your full contact information, a simple but significant gesture for two reasons:

- First, in order to do so, they must give you their e-mail address, enabling future non-intrusive communication.
- Second, you save them the distraction and time of writing down all your information, simultaneously guaranteeing they have a permanent and accurate record for you.

When e-mailing (your samples, or the URL for your website, etc.), most common formats will be friendly and the assistant will have no trouble opening your attachments in Word or the PDF format, etc. Nonetheless, it's simple, quick and thoughtful while on the phone to confirm that it's okay to send any document(s) you might have in other formats, should you have them, such as PowerPoint, text, or Excel. The last thing you want is to frustrate someone or cause a second round of communication about such non-essential details.

TAKE THE LONG VIEW

Don't push the envelope too quickly. Don't try too hard to be their friend and consume their precious time all at once. With each phone call (or e-mail), get that one next important piece of information. How long have they been at their present job, company? Are they originally from Los Angeles? Where'd they go to school? Are they in line or hoping to become an agent, producer, etc.?

Once you've established rapport and sense a 'relationship' building, ask if you can take them to lunch or meet for a coffee (likely on a weekend). Your treat! Ask how you might be helpful to them. Is there some way you can be of service or add value? It's likely they've never heard, let alone imagined, someone asking them that question.

The moral is simple: gently, thoughtfully, purposefully and with genuine interest, make the effort to grow every new relationship into a 'business friendship'.

GOOD CHOICES AND

THEIR BENEFITS

Remember, assistants hold the key to the kingdom. They can place your name and/or material at the top of their boss' list, bury it at the bottom, or simply toss it in the round file. They can ask their friends in the agency's talent department to introduce your materials to others, place your materials on the right desk, or maybe on the desk of their boss who's producing the project you've targeted for yourself.

The assistant can be your

> ### A GOLDEN NUGGET
>
> Whenever someone asks you to send them a treatment, I strongly urge you to ask instead that they read ten pages of your actual screenplay. It will take the exact same amount of time, but there's a world of difference. People request treatments only to avoid having to read an unknown writer's entire script.
>
> So see it for what it is, and don't automatically say 'yes' immediately. Politely, enthusiastically offer instead the first 10 pages of your script, with no obligation if they don't enjoy the read.
>
> Let them see how well you write an actual script, experience your 'voice' as a writer, which isn't as obvious from a treatment. No one buys a treatment, they buy scripts, which are an altogether different format and experience.
>
> So offer them the real deal and let them experience your craft as a professional screenwriter. They can't truly learn that from a treatment. The ten pages will give them a far better sense of your screenplay than any condensed treatment or synopsis, and is far more likely to 'hook' them. It's far more likely to increase the percentage of instances where your full screenplay is requested.

personal 'Merlin', creating opportunities and benefits you would likely not think of or be able to anticipate. The rewards of being courteous and friendly are profound in all areas of life. Nonetheless, good choices can pay disproportionate dividends in Hollywood.

It's surprising the many and varied rewards you will receive as a result of simply being respectful toward assistants and other 'lower echelon' folks in Hollywood - whether at agencies, productions companies, casting director offices or elsewhere. This is a general 'truism' in life and works magic, whether at your local bank or any other imaginable type of business where people tend to feel under-appreciated. You'll find many conversations and acts of goodwill occur 'behind your back' or out of your earshot.

I attribute a great deal of the good will I enjoy to my behaviors toward and relationships with assistants and other entry level personnel. Word of mouth and good rapport has helped in unexpected ways, often months or even years later. Please do not underestimate the power of simply honoring people by being friendly and respectful.

RELATIONSHIPS BEAR FRUIT

As a representative, I consistently introduced newer, less credentialed talent to lower level executives at production companies and major studios, as well as to casting directors, agencies and management companies. My experience on behalf of clients is filled with enduring, successful working relationships that blossomed from those young alliances. The success of clients who eventually were hired time and again can often be traced back to more humble beginnings. It's all about relationship. Just not necessarily relationship with the individual whose name appears on the company letterhead – at least not beginning on 'day one'.

And you can never tell just when the relationship will pay its dividend. Here's one of the many great stories I've accumulated along my journey:

When I was a personal manager, I'd been quite friendly with Ian, a successful literary agent at Triad, then a large agency in Los Angeles. Despite our rapport, I always made a habit of speaking with his assistant, Simon. Having developed a personal and professional friendship with Simon, I also made clear that he was the one to whom I would direct submissions. Though Ian would gladly have looked at material from my office, it served me, Simon and Ian well to take this approach. Ian looked at any material if Simon was enthusiastic; Simon was favorably disposed and felt empowered and accorded a special respect; and I had the benefit of two allies instead of one. We enjoyed a very successful collaboration over time. I continued to work with Simon when he left to become executive assistant to a top Hollywood producer, someone I got to know better as a direct result of my rapport with Simon.

More than 15 years later, a friend who happened to be a top chef in Los Angeles approached me for my advice. He'd just completed a manuscript and was seeking a first-rate publishing agent. I made some calls and every publishing agent I knew all recommended the very same authority in that niche. His name was Simon. He was acknowledged as best of breed in the New York publishing world. Simon's early education and subsequent stellar reputation and success in the publishing world was apparently well known.

I phoned Simon on behalf of my friend and, within moments of introducing myself, he asked if I was the same person he'd known from his days in the film business in Los Angeles. When he reminded me of who he'd worked with and how we met, I recalled Simon instantly. The next words out of his mouth were: "Whatever you need, whatever the reason for your call, I'll do absolutely anything I can to help you. You were the one person who took the time to get to know me, to really speak with me and listen to me, and I always appreciated you for that."

This was the very same person who years earlier was an assistant working an agent's desk, delivering packages to my and other people's offices and homes, and was now an extraordinarily well-connected and influential success in the inner sanctum of the New York publishing scene. Simon's is but one of countless similar success stories. The more value you add, the greater your bond early on in someone's career, the more likely you'll enjoy an enduring relationship for many years to come.

Assistants and others in Hollywood rise rapidly and matriculate in unexpected, non-linear directions. These micro-generations of new insiders are your potential 'power allies'. The greater your rapport with an assistant, the greater the long-term benefit of your relationship with them. The math of Hollywood may be less than obvious, but the calculus of a thoughtful strategy will yield significant results over time.

MY GATEKEEPERS

All of my former personal assistants have gone on to create their own remarkably successful careers. All remain friends. All beautifully illustrate how relationships with assistants become increasingly valuable over time.

Jennifer has enjoyed a successful 25+ year career spanning every aspect of the music business including work as a Warner Bros recording artist, touring as a keyboardist with Billy Idol and Savage Garden, among others, and becoming an A&R executive at Atlantic Records, Universal Publishing, Zomba Publishing, etc. For more than half a dozen years, Jennifer served as Senior VP at Universal Music Publishing Group in New York, where her roster included: Skylar Grey, Ne-Yo, Linkin Park, T-Pain, Justin Timberlake, Flyleaf, and Anthony Hamilton among others. She's an ASCAP writer herself, President of the New York Chapter of the Recording Academy, and is an Adjunct Professor at NYU.

Tricia went on to be one of the more respected casting directors in the business, successful both in television (e.g. *Dexter, The Gates, The Shield,* etc.) and feature films (*Twilight, The A-Team, Underworld,* etc.).

Kim formed Montage and grew it into the premier boutique agency representing the crème de la crème of photographers on the West Coast. It's hard to pick up a magazine today that doesn't feature one or more of her clients' artwork.

I grew to trust and rely in important ways on Jennifer, Tricia, Kim, and every assistant I've ever hired. Each of them proved themselves an enormous asset, filtering people and projects, looking out for my interests, sourcing opportunity and adding significant value to me and my company. Each of them had my ear and I listened when they were passionate and expressed enthusiasm or a point of view about a talent or project.

I assure you that if you invest in relationships with the gatekeepers, you invest in a future that tends to make success in Hollywood happen more quickly, with greater ease and more fun. See assistants as your greatest potential friends, mentors and allies, and you can shave **years** off your success curve. You'll also find 'the biz' doesn't always have to be or feel such a struggle.

THE IDEAL TIMES TO MAKE YOUR PHONE CALL

Assistants rarely frequent restaurants in the light of day. They're usually brown bagging it at their desk or running errands for their employer during 'lunch'.

'D' GATHERINGS

The assistant or other entry-level 'gatekeepers' are potentially not only your friend, but your greatest spokesperson.

Very common is a weekly 'pizza' night with a dozen other development execs ("d girls" or "d boys" as they were once commonly known) and/or assistants. Beyond gossip and general information exchange, they discuss all talent they've been introduced to during the preceding week.

This is their greatest currency. The writers, directors and actors they've discovered, the materials that stood out are their single greatest asset – and the quickest way they distinguish themselves. Bosses and peers alike pay keen attention and value enormously the discovery of new talent by an assistant or development executive. These 'discoveries' are the stuff of greater credibility and a forward momentum that propels them along their career path.

You want people mentioning you by name and speaking well of you in front of their peers. This is precisely the ripple effect you want.

You might not recognize it at the moment, but this is crucial information.

Hollywood business lunches are a tradition, a daily event beginning at 1 pm and ending normally by 2:30 pm (Los Angeles is in the Pacific time zone, as are all the times I'm referencing.) Travel time to the restaurant requires people leave their offices more or less 15 minutes earlier.

This means that an ideal time to phone an assistant is between 12:55 pm and 2:15 pm – after their boss has left for their lunch meeting, and before their return to the office. They may not be sitting at their desk the whole time, but if you find them on the phone during their boss' absence, the stress levels are noticeably lower, the phones ring less frequently, and the opportunity to engage and create rapport is tenfold greater.

If you reach voicemail, try again ten minutes or more later. There's a good chance the assistant has walked down the hall to the kitchen to retrieve or eat their lunch.

Another excellent time to phone the assistant is between 7:00 and 7:30 pm . The assistant generally stays at the office later than their boss, who frequently has scheduled an appointment for drinks or dinner. While people tend to be a bit more tired by that hour, it's still fertile phone time.

A third quality opportunity arises due to the fact that agents and most others in Hollywood normally attend one or more fairly lengthy (multi-hour) staff meetings each and every week. Once you've developed rapport with the assistant, it's worth casually inquiring when their boss has scheduled staff meetings. This allows you to intentionally design a more convenient and productive strategy. If you choose wisely (lunch, staff meeting, or evenings), the assistant will be less distracted and your communication will be less hectic.

The same applies whether contacting assistants to managers or producers or agents. The 1:00 pm lunch is standard fare for all. The staff meeting may be a bit more specific to agencies, management companies and studios.

LOST ART OF THE HAND-WRITTEN NOTE

On the second or third call, casually ask the assistant their birthday and mark it on your calendar. Even if you've lost contact, mail a brief hand-written note to each person in your ever-growing Rolodex – assistants and others - to celebrate them on their birthday. This small personal gesture will make even the most jaded person feel wonderful, and you will be remembered for it. Hand-written notes have become rare in today's world, and thus are all the more special and appreciated. Please avoid email, fax or text messaging. You want to stand out and not merely be another item in someone's in-box.

Whenever the assistant goes out of their way to assist you, write to express your appreciation. Write a thank you note for any effort you feel is thoughtful and meaningful. Acknowledge them if they:

- Reviewed and responded to any materials you submitted,
- Passed your resume along to their boss,
- Introduced you to a friend or colleague at the same or a different company, or
- Shared with you a critical piece of information.

The same holds true for anyone, not merely assistants. Being courteous, professional and thoughtful will make you feel good, and people will take notice and appreciate you in return. Little gestures make big statements.

MILESTONES

Be Respectful And Make A Friend

- Learn the names of every assistant you speak with and make them your allies.
- Introduce yourself, make certain it's a convenient time for them to speak, state your business, seek their advice, be concise, offer to email them all your contact information.
- Whenever possible, conduct your business with the assistant; do not needlessly attempt to get their boss on the phone; address all your questions to the assistant, making them your principal contact.
- Ask permission to address the assistant directly with any resume, writing samples, or other item.
- Phone at strategic times when the boss is likely away from his or her desk and the assistant's stress levels are lower.

Submitting Materials

- Make every assistant — to an agent, manager, producer or director —your ally by

- getting to know them over the phone, asking if they (_not their boss_) will review your materials first.
- Empower the assistant. Always. You will likely be the only one that day who is wise enough to do so.
- Set the tone for a relationship where the assistant will be motivated to help you in the moment, and you will continue to serve each other's career goals. You will find you become long-time colleagues with many assistants over time.

So far you've been on your own in this process – networking, branding yourself, developing both your D. O. lists and your relationships with the assistants of the Hollywood world. Now it's time to start adding some players to the team.

Next chapter? Building Your Dream Team.

SUCCESS STRATEGY FIVE: BUILDING YOUR DREAM TEAM

Creating Your Inner Circle

Teamwork is so important that it is virtually impossible for you to reach the heights of your capabilities or make the money that you want without becoming very good at it.

~ Brian Tracy, author and business coach

No person in any field of endeavor creates great and enduring success all alone. Writing is a business, your field of endeavor, and your business requires and deserves a talented and experienced team to help plan and accelerate your success.

Agents and managers are critical members of your team as you build a strong foundation for your career as a writer. Your team may grow to include an attorney and others, but representation by a quality agent and/or manager is vital. The manager and agent are part of your master plan, the very people who will guide, promote and grow your relationships, fan base and career. They champion your work and widen your sphere of influence.

If you have one or the other already on your team, excellent. If not, this will be an early priority and this book will provide you the tools and strategies to research, communicate with and understand what type of agent and/or manager is best suited to you. The search for a qualified and appropriate representative will simply become part of your daily action plan.

For reasons discussed below, it may be more likely and realistic to begin by securing representation by a manager. The manager can subsequently help you find an agent.

Nonetheless, don't think in terms of agent versus manager, but rather in terms of quality, enthusiasm, reputation, and the person who most clearly communicates a thoughtful strategic approach and plan *for you*. As you add members to your team, you'll just continue to increase your opportunity for quality introductions and meetings.

THAT'S NICE, BUT HOW DO I GET THEIR ATTENTION?

Referrals.

Yes, you can and should research and create a targeted list of the representatives you think would be a huge win for you (maybe you've already included them on your top 100 list that you developed in the first chapter on networking). You might want to begin a campaign of calling them (better, their assistants) and submitting your materials and making yourself known to them.

But the shortest distance between wanting a quality agent or manager and actually being signed by one is simple: *get referrals.*

If you surveyed the majority of agents and managers, asking how they came to represent their current clients, their responses would be a chorus of 'referral'. The vast majority of signed writing clients get in the door initially because someone known, liked and trusted by the agent (or manager) sent them, referred them, talked them up. That's the case 95% of the time, if not more.

The same holds true in every walk of life in Hollywood. As a manager and later as a producer, a minimum of 95% of all my clients and/or projects came to my attention because of referrals. This was true for potential clients (i.e., talent) and for potential projects (i.e., screenplays, books etc.).

How did this 95% come about? Someone on my staff (my assistant or development team) or a friend in the business made an enthusiastic recommendation. Since these are people I trust and respect, people who know me and my taste, I take their endorsements and referrals seriously. It doesn't matter what hat they wear, so long as I respect them professionally.

Referrals came from all directions, some expected, e.g., agents, managers, actors, other writers, directors, studio executives, talent coordinators, and many very unexpected sources, e.g., cinematographers, photographers, line producers, attorneys, sales agents, and often from their assistants. The only constant was that someone I knew was giving their seal of approval, essentially lending their credibility and reputation, in support of a new talent I'd not previously known.

I would take meetings, read screenplays, take phone calls, do whatever was necessary to discover a brilliant new talent, but generally only if recommended or referred by a trusted colleague. Why? Because I only have so many hours in the day. But if someone I like had filtered that opportunity or person, that justified me investing my precious time. And that's just the way it works.

THE TRICK...ASK!

All you have to do is ask. This is the lesson we talked about in the Networking chapter. Ask people for their guidance, counsel, suggestions. Ask people you instinctively like and respect, whether you met them in an writing class, at the coffee shop, at the gym, at a networking event. What is their experience with agents and managers? Would they be willing to share your scripts with their agent's assistant? Maybe it's not as bold as asking for a meeting, but rather to seek another professional opinion about your treatment. Whatever is within people's comfort zone and gets the job done. That's the obvious route.

Less obvious can be more effective. Whenever I was approached by someone I liked – a photographer, the assistant to a casting director, or a cinematographer – I always felt I was getting an inside tip and early opportunity from an unlikely source. I paid attention. Consider approaches and pathways that are less travelled, and thus more innovative and original and surprising. You never know who knows who. You can't know who will be activist and enthusiastic, a potential pipeline to a future member of your professional team.

So don't judge or be shy. The entire world, including your life map of relationships (the majority of whom are not even in the entertainment world), are nothing if not opportunities for counsel and introductions.

J.F. Lawton, a writer I managed and produced, was the screenwriter responsible for both *Pretty Woman* and the original *Under Siege*. Had I not listened to the person who recommended I read his work and meet him, those films and successes would have been lost.

So if you want to speed your way to conversations and meetings with quality agents and managers, seek out 'referrals'. The fastest way to turn a 'no' to a 'yes' is to utilize what we know to be true about human nature.

AGENTS, MANAGERS AND THE WRITER BREAKING IN

The agent and the manager are both engaged in the business of representing individual creative careers, but there are significant differences.

As a general rule of thumb, agents tend to live within a very specific economic model: they're encouraged to sign income-producing clients. If you're not a proven talent with established commercial (earnings) history, or don't hold the promise of producing significant income rather quickly, the vast majority of agents are less likely to 'sign' you.

The big four agencies are:

- Creative Artists Agency
- William Morris Endeavor
- International Creative Management
- United Talent Agency

There are many other established, respected mid-size agencies, all of whom you can research using the resources described later in this chapter. There are also many quality, albeit slightly smaller, 'boutique' agencies. Several good examples of mid-size agencies might include:

- Paradigm
- The Gersh Agency
- Innovative Artists

SIZE-WISE

All of these agencies require good business incentive to sign a client. An agent at one of these larger or mid-size companies almost always needs to achieve consensus within their literary department before being approved to sign a new client. This is true despite the reality the client will conduct their business primarily or only with the one agent who signs them.

One of the defining distinctions separating agency from management is the size of their client list. An individual agent will often be responsible for 50 to 60 clients. A manager is more likely to have far fewer clients to service on a daily basis, perhaps 15 per manager. The size of the firm overall is then a function of the number of agents, each with an average number of clients. (As a rule of thumb, the larger the firm – whether an agency or a management company – the greater the need for consensus in signing a client.)

As a pragmatic and philosophical matter, managers focus not only on servicing the careers of more established clients, but also on discovering and developing the careers of newer talent. An exciting writer is grist for a manager's mill, despite the reality that it will take some time to develop that career to the point of becoming a reliable income stream.

As a general rule, most agencies, including the more modestly-sized companies, are not necessarily in the business of finding, discovering, nurturing, and developing new talent. They're bookers. Even some of the more mature or 'muscular' management companies will devote less resource to developing new talent.

In general, however, the management model is more inclined toward long term career development, and where professionally newer writers will more readily succeed in securing early representation.

FINDING THE RIGHT KEY FOR THE RIGHT DOOR

Whether targeting agents or managers, marketing is key. Being determined and disciplined, being your own best chief marketing officer and sales team will have every bit as much to do with your results as your talent. Initiate calls and reach out to make new relationships every day. Produce amazing scripts that stand out, and generally be imaginative and tireless in pursuit of your dreams. Enjoy doing something every day to improve your reach and relationships. Do for yourself the exact things you'll soon be asking your agent and/or manager to do on your behalf. Learn to enjoy, make a fun challenge, be consistent as your own Chief Marketing Officer. Those who do are rewarded with measurable results, those who don't wonder why they haven't been discovered yet.

Find your way more quickly into quality meetings with agents and managers, producers and executives. Prospective representatives will find you more attractive precisely because you're an activist as a marketer on your own behalf. Marketing 'savvy' is the one thing that most dramatically separates you from other equally talented writers.

For a manager who's open to working with 'green' talent, the search criteria are simple:

- strong craft and a unique creative 'voice', and
- the intelligence and personality to be well-received (and to make for a pleasant and successful representative-client relationship).

If you've not been represented before and you don't have a long list of credits, that's probably less important than having a winning personality and presence, obvious talent, and an unshakeable belief in yourself and a willingness to do whatever it takes. For many managers, it's incredibly exciting to discover a writer of extraordinary talent to unveil to the world.

The newer writer may offer some real and perceived advantages from the manager's perspective as well. If the talent is evident, the writer comes to the relationship with no 'baggage' or history that might complicate matters. There will be no surprises, only the excitement of introducing their latest discovery… you.

DEFINITIONS AND DIFFERENCES

Unlike managers, agents and agencies tend to be state regulated. According to California state statute, it is the jurisdiction of the agent "to solicit and negotiate" work on behalf of artists. Talent agents fall under the rubric of 'employment agents', an area clearly defined by state labor codes. Technically, a manager would violate such state law by seeking employments or making contracts for same on behalf of clients.

While technically not permitted to solicit work or negotiate deals, most managers ignore that dictum and actively promote their clients. In practice, it's exceedingly rare that anyone would complain, so long as fair and professional behaviors are the norm. A client who benefits from the services of a manager would have little reason to be upset.

Regulated by their state bar association, attorneys are not 'employment agents', and also enjoy great license and are perfectly able and entitled to submit your work for consideration and to negotiate deals.

Agents are legally allowed to charge and collect a maximum commission of ten percent of a client's gross earnings. That is the norm and will be clearly spelled out in the agency agreement.

Unlike agents, managers are not subject to state regulation, yet also earn their income by charging and collecting a commission of a client's gross revenues. The range is not codified, but as a practice will be in ten to fifteen percent range. If there's an agent and manager, it would be less common to see a manager's commission exceed ten percent. This is different than music or other entertainment arenas where commissions for managers can be significantly higher. By the same token, a client with a highly successful career and income can negotiate a lower (e.g. five percent) commission structure.

THE FLOW OF MONEY

While commission-based agents and managers work for free until such time as you realize income, it often comes as a surprise to writers when their gross check is reduced by two or more commissions (possibly another five percent to an attorney), slashed again by taxes, yielding a far smaller amount than they might have imagined. In the end, effective representation will build your career and your 'price' in the marketplace. Nonetheless, plan well and don't spend your anticipated earnings prematurely.

Once you have signed an agreement to be represented by either an agent and/or a manager, you are bound to pay commissions, even if you (and/or your contacts) created the opportunity.

Monies due you for work will be remitted by the production company or studio to your representative, generally the agent of record if you have one. Accompanied by a statement, those funds may then be forwarded to your manager (or to you directly if you do not have a manager), less the agency commission which will have been retained by the agency. If you have a manager and no agent, initial payment will generally be directed to your manager.

WHAT CAN YOU EXPECT FROM A MANAGER OR AGENT?

A passionate, professional, enthusiastic representative offers encourage-ment, educates the writer-client, and preaches their client's unique merits to all who will listen. They take to heart their client's needs and desires, fighting daily battles, suffering rejections and frustrations with and on be-half of the client and, occasionally if not frequently, celebrating with them skirmishes won, taking small but significant steps ever closer to their goals.

The following describes a host of different functions that may be han-dled or supplemented by the efforts of your agent and/or manager. Where both an agent and manager exist, the manager-client relationship is often thought to be more close-knit, but neither is inherently more important. Both can and should be viewed as vital, once the choice is made to have them on board.

Introducing you and your work to the community

Submitting your screenplays and teleplays to producers, directors, networks and others; these professionals accept your materials from credible agents or managers far more readily than from you directly.

Broadening your contacts

This may include general or pitch meetings; introducing or recommending script consultants; agents introducing you to managers or vice versa; as well as possibly encouraging or inviting you to attend certain 'business-social' events such as screenings or guild-sponsored luncheons.

Assembling the best possible 'team' for you

Your manager should seek the best possible agent for you. If you have an agent and desire a manager, the same holds true in reverse. Each should be responsive to and encouraging of additional representation if that is your desire. If so, they should submit your materials and set meetings with prospective representatives they respect and with whom they've enjoyed successful experience in the past.

A quality entertainment attorney is another enormous value and, at some point, you will want one on your team. Your agent and/or manager can help with that introduction and selection process as well. (We'll be discussing this in more detail in the next chapter.)

Identifying appropriate work opportunities

This would include all projects and meetings that align with your agreed-upon career goals. These opportunities can span films, TV series, stage plays and beyond.

Acting as your personal creative affairs department

Masterminding ideas for everything from your next project to possibly introducing potential collaborators if you desire to develop other content.

Making the client aware of upcoming projects

Agents and managers can often introduce you to projects well in advance of their going into active production.

Providing in-house business affairs support

In early negotiations and deal structuring, your agent may save you the potential cost of an attorney (which may be a future commission, rather than an hourly cash fee). Depending on the complexity of the deal and your agent's negotiating and/or drafting skills, an attorney may be a smart investment in the long run. Over time, you will want a seasoned entertainment attorney as a key member of your team. Although some managers may be quite adept, they are technically precluded from negotiating deals.

Project support a/k/a Packaging

Some agencies, depending on their size, can help you 'package' your project. The same goes for a manager, who is free to approach multiple agencies (not just the one you're signed with, assuming you have an agent) with the same goal in mind. Each 'element' (whether a director or a well-regarded foreign sales agent, etc.) helps attract the other essential ingredients.

Similarly, they may be able to provide feedback or story notes for your project, as well as help attract or secure financing, distribution or other strategic or creative elements or partners.

Helping create cross-over opportunity

You may wish to cross-over into a different medium (e.g. from feature film to series television, or vice-versa), which requires a different set of relationships and a strategy to cross that divide.

Publicity

Creating, screening, avoiding and/or managing public relations will more likely be the task of the manager.

Troubleshooting

Handling any difficulties that may arise vis-a-vis a client's relationships with studios and/or producers is a function likely shared by agent and manager (if both exist).

This is by no means an exhaustive list and much will depend on your unique needs as a client, but the foregoing covers a majority of the usual activities and benefits that can flow from agent/manager relationships.

ESTABLISHING A LONG-TERM SUCCESSFUL

RELATIONSHIP

First and foremost, your representative is your chief strategist, your chief operating officer, your greatest advocate. But while he or she should be a constant activist on your behalf, it's also important you continue to engage and participate fully in managing your career and its trajectory. You'll continue to network, continue refining your brand with your team, and continue developing those relationships – all the strategies we have talked about that transform your career goals into achievable results.

When trying to decide if a particular agent or manager is a good match for you, listen carefully and you'll quickly get a sense of the person's ability to analyze your career and the business in general. There are representatives whose style is somewhat more random and there are those whose approach is logical, well thought out and susceptible of being communicated clearly to the client. Look for the intelligent game plan. At a minimum, make certain there is a game plan and your potential representative has the necessary cachet or access, and not just belief.

Get a clear sense of how the agent or manager will handle themselves on your behalf within the larger community. You want to be represented in a way that reflects well on you.

Your career is a business and you want someone on your team who thinks and understands how to move you closer to your goals. The more specific you are, the more specific the dialogue can become. Spell out as much as you can and then listen intently to the agent or manager's strategy. Engage your brain, trust your instincts, and choose wisely.

When entering into a new relationship with a manager or agent, disclose all existing relationships and a full history of meetings whether good or bad. This information avoids any information gaps or embarrassment.

Similarly, if you have a short 'wish list' of individuals or companies you'd like to meet, communicate those desires. The agent or manager may agree or may offer thoughtful reasons why that strategy is not ideal in the short term.

Set the tone from the very beginning of your relationship to manage expectations, maintain energy and momentum, and create a pattern of healthy and intelligent dialogue.

LIKE CLOCKWORK

From the outset, initiate a pattern of one brief, focused, regular weekly conversation with your agent and/or manager to update one another, and keep each other abreast of new people, meetings and opportunities. For lesser details or when confirming information, a call to the assistant or the use of email is usually more convenient and effective.

This governed and predictable approach insures continuity and a stronger relationship over time. Calling a few times a week is not appropriate unless you are in the middle of an active negotiation or other time-sensitive event.

Make sure you prepare for each week's call, and that you've organized your thoughts and questions; apply the lessons of your D. O. list in getting ready for this call. Aim to keep your calls between five and ten minutes.

> **DON'T FORGET THE**
>
> **ASSISTANT!**
>
> Even though you'll be doing your weekly check-in call with your agent or manager, make sure to get in the routine of placing a separate quick (five-minutes, tops) call to their assistant. Remember, this is a separate (if parallel) relationship you are developing, and these weekly calls will not only benefit you in the short term, but in the future as well.

Your agent or manager may wish or need to phone you more frequently, whether to follow up on a meeting, let you know when another is being scheduled, or give you background on the people that will be in the room for your upcoming meeting. On the other hand, their assistant is more than capable to communicate with you about directions or addresses, names, etc.. The goal is simply never to allow a couple of weeks or more to pass without a brief conversation.

Common sense is the rule. Make yourself the client that is always smart, charming, enjoyable, getting to the point quickly. Don't simply ask what's being done on your behalf. Let your representative know any new relationships you've initiated, and any other relevant information. Make the relationship productive and fun.

Feel free to ask questions. It's an essential part of your education. Avoid the pitfall of the passive client who lets his or her career be choreographed without having a great deal to say in the matter. This will insure you continue to enjoy a greater *sympatico* and that your goals are not lost in the mix. Help your agent or manager create the game plan, then leave her or him to execute it.

Many writers seem to feel lucky to have a representative and adopt a semi-passive posture vis-à-vis their agent and/or manager. Better to be activist, pick their brains, learn at every opportunity while not consuming unnecessary amounts of time. The more you contribute ideas, information and relationships, the better. It will be appreciated and evidence of your full commitment.

THE TEAM THAT PLAYS WELL TOGETHER

Be realistic in assessing periodically the style and value and contribution of each member of your team. Make certain they're working well together as a team, sharing information, coordinating efforts and equally active.

For example, you don't want a manager who simply phones the agent every day, inquiring what the agent has or has not done that day. This will not be well-received by the agent, nor does it serve you well.

A good team will strategize together, choose who is the more effective negotiator, who has the better relationship with a particular casting director or producer.

LONG TERM, SHORT TERM

The manager often takes a more long-term view of a writer's career, always keeping the larger canvas in mind and making certain that each choice helps steer a particular course.

In the long term, agency should be viewed as an essential relationship. For the writer who already enjoys a good agent relationship, the notion of a manager may begin to lose merit. Yet, you are the only one who can define your goals and progress toward those goals in the overall context of your career. There are some truly excellent agents who comport themselves like a manager, expending more time per client than one might expect.

Answers to the following types of questions may help you assess your representation, or your need of new or additional representation.

- Are you getting regular meetings for the kind of quality projects that satisfy you?
- Are you meeting with or beginning to collaborate with the caliber of directors, producers, other writers that excite you?
- Are you and your materials regularly exposed to the appropriate caliber of people within the producing and creative community?
- Does your representative offer you smart feedback and creative input?
- Is your representative fiercely honest with you, providing candid feedback – good or bad – from meetings?
- Is your representative's follow-through consistent, timely and effective?
- Are your relationships, meetings and opportunities progressively increasing in number and quality?
- Subject to realistic expectations and the game plan you agreed upon when you signed with your representation, are you hitting your marks economically?
- Are your agent and/or manager working as enthusiastically and consistently as they did at the outset?

These are just examples of questions you may want to consider over time, perhaps even before you sign with a representative. Know whether you share similar and realistic expectations about the relationship and your respective goals and work styles. It's your career and those entrusted with representing you (including agent, manager and attorney) are there to serve you and your goals.

CREDIBLE REPRESENTATION

As a general maxim, you should rarely pay monies for any professional services pertaining to your career. An obvious exception would be attorneys, who may be paid on an hourly basis or by commission.

Never agree to be represented by an agency that attempts to charge you any sort of fee other than a fixed maximum ten percent commission on your writing-related income.

Be wary of agents or managers who advertise in newspapers and industry trade publications, or ones who over-promise you results. Legitimate representatives are not in the habit of taking out advertisements in any publication (other than congratulatory ads in trade magazines).

BE A SLEUTH

It's important and quite simple to un-earth information about a potential representative. It's always advisable to do some homework about their clients, relationships, job history, standing and achievements. A quick search of Google, and especially of articles in the trade papers (e.g. The Hollywood Reporter or Deadline), should give you all the information you need.

In addition to news clippings, articles, and a host of directories, many of which are free, there are a variety of free and paid websites that can deliver valuable information.

One of the most popular sites is Internet Movie Data Base. This service offers a free version and a paid or premium service as well. The paid service provides significantly more data and detail on people and projects.

Agencies and management companies are generally ferociously protective of and will rarely divulge their 'client list'. There are numerous reasons for secrecy. Nonetheless, there are many ways to gather intelligence and fairly assess individual agents and managers, as well as the companies as a whole, and even the makeup of their client list. This is true not just for writers, but for actors and directors as well.

In your quest for information on the best representation for you and your career, you should also actively pursue online writer forums and community groups. Join chat rooms and seek out free memberships in the various writer 'bulletin boards' online. It's a great way to get advice, as long as you're aware that advice may come from seasoned writers with a great deal of experience, or from inexperienced writers who simply think they know more than they do.

ONCE YOU HAVE AN AGENT OR MANAGER…THEN WHAT?

Do not stop being your own best advocate and activist. Do not subvert your will or common sense. Be flexible, communicative and respectful with your representative, keeping them up to date *vis-à-vis* your activities. Representatives appreciate a client who brings quality contacts to bear on their own career.

The only thing you **do not want to do** is continue submitting your materials directly. That should be left for your agent and/or manager. If you meet someone who expresses interest in you, let them know your agent/manager will forward them your materials. Then simply phone or email your representative the intended recipient's contact information (name, company, address and phone) and allow them to do the legwork. It will avoid confusion between you and your representative(s), and allow you to maintain your enthusiastic creative persona, never sullying yourself with the business of the business.

Enjoy the best of both worlds, having effective representation and yet forging ahead by your own actions. The two will complement one another and add up to something greater than either might alone.

MILESTONES

- Know your reps: Agents are state regulated, authorized to solicit work and negotiate on your behalf. Managers tend toward a more long-term view and often are more prone to developing newer talent.

- Know the essential functions of an agent and/or manager, which are to:
  - Broaden your contacts through meetings and submissions.
  - Seek out employment opportunities.
  - Offer you creative notes and feedback.
  - Help attract talent and possible financing to your project.
  - Act as your business affairs person (for negotiations and contracts).
  - Expand your team (manager finds agent or vice versa).
- Know how to manage your relationship with your agent or manager with weekly brief, informative phone conversations.
- Research agencies and management firms (and individual agents and managers) through trade publications, websites, professional directories or Google. Check press clippings relating to any agency or agent, management company or manager you are considering or with whom you are meeting.
- Participate and ask questions in online writer forums to identify or get more information about specific agencies or management companies.
- Look for a smaller or mid-size firm that can offer you the quality of attention you seek for your career.
- Avoid agencies or management companies that advertise in newspapers or that charge any fee other than a commission on earned income.

So far you've networked your way into connecting with lots of people – assistants especially; you've focused on your brand, so you know the career trajectory you have in mind, and now you have the professional support to help you. Then next step is demonstrating your professionalism by getting you and your work the legal protection and representation you both deserve.

SUCCESS STRATEGY SIX: GET SMART, GET LEGAL, GET PROTECTED

How To Avoid Potholes, Protect Your Work and Your Career

God is love, but get it in writing.

~ Gypsy Rose Lee

Imagine you wake up tomorrow, you just finished your first cup of coffee and the phone rings. You pick up the phone and hear one of the following extraordinary bits of exciting news…

- Paul Producer just finished reading your most recent script and wants to option it immediately; or
- Eddie Executive from Significant Studio just came out of a staff meeting and has the group's blessing – after everyone read your latest screenplay over the weekend – to move forward and purchase your screenplay; or
- Bonnie Boxoffice tells you she was blown away by your pitch last week and they now want you to write their project on assignment;

Or you pick up the phone and learn one of the following bits of possibly-maybe-also-very-good-news…

- Isabelle at Indie Prod Company, Inc. loves your project and, with exuberance and enthusiasm, describes their plan to package and set up your film, but they'll need *a six month free option*; or
- On the heels of your brainstorm session yesterday with your good friend Scott Screenwriter, his representative Mary Manager calls to

congratulate you on the brilliant idea you and her client *co-created* and that you're about to write as a team. She's certain it's the most commercial idea she's heard in ages and can't wait until it's completed so she can sell it for beaucoup bucks; or

- Alan Assistant who works for the head of film packaging at the second biggest agency in the industry tells you he knows exactly who is looking for the specific story you've written – it's a very big name director-actor-producer-or-studio head <u>and</u> his boss will support this project <u>100%</u> if you'll just give him *a short exclusive window* to make it happen; or

- Your friendly development executive, Walter Wannabee from Phantom Film Factory phones to tell you that if you'll just do one revision to *incorporate their notes*, his boss is willing to option your script (rare though it may be, you actually loved their creative notes and think they'll improve your script).

Welcome to the labyrinth, where so many have gotten a bit disoriented and lost their way. This is the labyrinth of rights, options, registrations and the various distinctions when creating and managing *intellectual property* (affectionately known as IP).

These are some of the key questions we're going to address in this chapter:

- What sort of monies and other terms do you ask for in an option? For how long?
- How do you determine the value of your work if someone wants to purchase it?
- If someone is impressed by your writing and wants you to write an assignment as a 'work for hire', do you merely accept 'guild minimum' payment? And what about credit?
- Under what circumstances, if any, would you be willing to grant a free option?
- You and a writing partner are excited about collaborating on a new idea. Does it matter that your partner is already represented? Why would you need an agreement and what issues would it address?
- What restrictions and guidelines, if any, would give you the comfort to give an exclusive 'window' to a big-wig to shop your material?

- How can you incorporate any content, ideas or material from another person into your script without jeopardizing the future of your work?
- When do I need to copyright and/or register my script?

What do you do?
Who do you call?
Who can you turn to for guidance?

THE RULES

You're going to call your dream team, of course, and if your team doesn't yet include an attorney, you'll be adding to the team. But before we get to the appropriate responses to these calls, let's review a few rules first, because flattering calls or interested inquiries about your script can lead to momentary brain freeze. And before we talk about getting legal and getting protected, there are some basic rules that we have to go over – i.e., getting smart.

First Rule of the Jungle:
   Never ever agree to anything that is not reduced to writing.
   Repeat after me: *Never, ever, never, ever* agree to anything that is NOT reduced to writing
   … AND signed by BOTH parties.
   It matters not who's on the other end of the conversation. An agreement or memorandum or contract, laying forth the essential terms and signed by both sides, is a must! Every time. Else you can look forward to a stunning disappointment and, in the bargain, appear less than professional and, albeit unwittingly, more likely to invite others to take advantage. Your generosity and trusting spirit can only get you in trouble. An agreement need not be a thick sheaf of paperwork. I prefer very short, clear and concise memos that eliminate the possibility for confusion or conflict, and address issues and solutions to avoid future disagreement or stalemates.
   Here's the problem.
   No matter how impeccable, honorable and well-intended your prospective producer (financier, director, sales agent, distributor, or anyone else you may be in discussions with), they are just the first stop on a longer journey.

If optioning your screenplay to a producer, the nature of the business makes it inevitable you and the producer will have different interests or points of view at some future date. Even if your interests coincide, it's not their responsibility to protect you if and when a distributor or financier wants to cut your fee, replace you, not allow or fund you to go on location during filming, or otherwise undermine what you felt was your understanding.

Whether in film or TV, success is a long and highly collaborative process, involving the passage of time and many people (and that means fuzzy memories that may not reliably or accurately recall the details of an oral agreement made some time ago).

Human nature, memories and business mandates are unpredictable and often suffer 'selective recall'.

Whether you're optioning a book, optioning or selling your screenplay, agreeing to co-author a screenplay, or innocently and enthusiastically agreeing to include a producer or director's ideas or notes into your existing material, take care to set out your agreement in writing to eliminate any potential misunderstanding down the road. Make certain it's signed by both parties, and each keeps an original for their files.

It is not an adversarial energy and never need be an adversarial process. Rather it's respectful and professional. Your tone is easy, transparent, confident, friendly. Be the one to offer to create a memo to support this new relationship and your shared goals. By doing so, you stay in control of the process and avoid reacting to paperwork created by someone else's attorney or agent. Remember, it's always happiest during the honeymoon, so that's the time to create a signed agreement. Once done, you move forward with clarity and peace of mind. Attempting to document a relationship or agenda long after the ship has sailed can be challenging at best, and sometimes simply impossible.

This first rule is sacred. I've witnessed too many projects run aground, seen promising relationships ruined, watched far too much quality material buried forever simply for want of a signed understanding. *He said, she said* is a dismal future for your intellectual property, one that all-too-often leads to burial in the IP graveyard that's littered with countless years of hard work by talented writers who simply didn't know the value of a signed, written agreement

And it's not just for your own sake or the future of this particular project. It's so you preserve happy, healthy relationships with everyone going forward. Remember, success is not project-based, it's relationship-based, so you want to protect each and every one going forward.

And it's the right and fair approach. Your producer invests, in every sense of the word, to add value and ready your project for production. It often takes years to assemble the elements: talent, financing, director, cast, distribution and so on. So you're not the only person you will be protecting along the way.

An important fact to realize: *Anyone unwilling to sign a proper memo of understanding is not someone with whom you would want to enter into a business relationship anyway.*

Second Rule of the Jungle

You never work for free, unless there are extreme and compelling reasons, AND you've observed Rule # 1 (the conditions of that work are spelled out in a signed writing).

As a professional writer, try to always receive value for your work, and do not create a habit or expectation that you perform work for free. If you perform work for free *on occasion*, make certain the quality of the people, the strategy, and the creative changes all justify you performing work for free in that particular instance.

Then, if you must work for free, *a written agreement – even with no dollars changing hands – is still an absolute requirement…* there's every bit as much at stake as if this was a paid writing assignment or someone was optioning your screenplay, and you should protect yourself, your IP and your future with every bit as much care.

Beyond the terms or understanding of everyone's role and rights and compensation should the project go forward, there are issues to clarify even if the project does not go forward with that particular producer or team. A central question most overlooked is who has rights vis-à-vis any material or ideas you add into your own script – whether it's a first draft or a rewrite of your existing script – that were suggested by another, regardless of whether or not you are getting paid.

Third Rule of the Jungle

Never ever speak business on your own behalf.

You are the eternally thoughtful, charming, creative, happy, open-minded, easy-to-get-along-with, super-talented and very fast writer *they* (the powers that be) love bringing in for meetings and who *they* should be so lucky to hire, or whose work *they* should be so lucky to option, purchase, finance and produce.

You're relaxed, confident, smile a lot and express continuous enthusiasm, but you agree to nothing... other than you think it sounds amazing and you'll be back in touch very soon.

So who do you call for advice? What are your choices?

Your friend who's a slightly more seasoned or successful screenwriter?

NO, unless it's to get a referral to his or her agent or attorney.

An agent? Possibly.

A manager? Also a candidate.

An attorney? Another really good idea.

> **RULE RE-CAP**
>
> With the sole exception of you writing alone on spec – i.e. with input from no one else – every other writing arrangement requires, deserves, and needs to be clear and committed to paper.
>
> A signed writing (rule #1) that includes payment (rule #2) and is negotiated on your behalf by an agent, manager and/or attorney (rule #3)...these are the ground rules that, if obeyed, insure you a happier and more successful future.

CALL YOUR A-TEAM

If you have a manager and/or agent and/or attorney, it's fairly obvious. Inform anyone and everyone already on your team and decide collectively how to handle the situation and who will take the lead. Managers are not allowed by California state statute to solicit or negotiate deals, so, while they can advise, they ultimately would need bring on board or refer you to an agent or attorney... at least in theory (truth be told, many managers will assume that role – especially if you have no other representative).

Some agents are amazingly excellent and strategic dealmakers. Some are not. Know which you have or are meeting with.

If you have either an agent or manager, make the call. Remembering back to when you signed on with that agent or manager, you should have discussed openly how you would work together, your respective ideas and styles and goals. One of your stated goals (again, ideally so) was to have your representative introduce you to their top choice of attorney (or possibly two or three so you could find the one you had the best understanding and chemistry with).

If that hasn't happened yet, this would be the perfect moment to expand your team and bring on board a smart attorney, who'll be crucial to your long-term success. Use the momentum and energy of outside interest in your project to entice people to meet with you. Activity makes people interested, makes them believe your talent is now ready to translate to real, ongoing income, i.e., *a stream of commissions for them.*

RECRUIT YOUR A-TEAM

If you have no attorney, no agent, no manager, then it's time to get a referral to quality legal representation, even if only for purposes of helping manage your current need.

When asking an agent, manager, producer, another screenwriter or anyone else for a referral to or recommendation for an attorney, you ideally want someone who:

- is respected as a skilled negotiator and dealmaker;
- has a great client list (i.e. is in demand and in constant communication with everyone in town); and
- enjoys a reputation for fiercely protecting his or her clients.

QUALITY, ENTHUSIASM, CAPACITY AND VISION

The more quality people on your team, the better. Anyone worth bringing on your team must first and foremost be someone you're convinced has a plan, has the capacity to execute that plan on your behalf, and is sufficiently enthusiastic they'll stay the course.

You don't want to compromise and have someone represent you that reflects badly on you. Over time, you'll meet quality agents and managers and attorneys, and you'll want to choose team members that are best for you and your goals. Opinions will differ, but if you have the happy problem of meeting, doing due diligence on, and having a choice to be represented by multiple representatives, my view is simple: more is better.

It's that many more voices out in the community talking about you, that many more clients they represent that you could gain access to, that many more referrals and relationships you'll be able to access across the town, and that much more information coming into their brains that can directly benefit you. I believe agents, managers and attorneys bring immense value simply if they're talking about you, circulating your work, being your goodwill ambassador. Most clients get their own work, meaning people hire you because they like you and they like your work. But the connective

SOME GOOD QUESTIONS TO ASK ABOUT ATTORNEYS

- Is she or he thorough and professional?
- What is their reputation in the community?
- Are they generous with general strategic advice and/or intro-ductions to other clients or relationships in general?
- Who are their other clients?
- What's the culture of the office? Do they treat their assistant well? • Is it relatively easy to contact them directly? How quickly are your phone calls returned?

tissue is often your team, whose individual and collective efforts on your behalf cause a groundswell of conversation and awareness. When it comes time to make a deal – or avoid a potentially bad situation – they can be worth their weight in gold.

Early on, I would not suggest targeting attorneys at really large law firms. Just like agents at the four big agencies, attorneys at the larger firms may not be ideal for you until you're really well established and can be the tail that wags the dog. I prefer writers seek out an attorney with a brilliant reputation who is either a sole practitioner or is part of a boutique or more modestly-sized firm.

In a perfect world, I'd have all your representatives participate, give advice, talk to each other, and arrive at a strategy, including who will be the one to speak on your behalf – and that would have to be either the agent or attorney.

If you've yet to form a relationship with any form of representative, attorney included, please refer back to the strategies discussed in the chapter on networking and in building your dream team. Ask everyone you respect, be they a writer, script consultant, actor, development executive, assistant to an agent, members of online forums, guild offices, absolutely anyone you believe may lead you to be introduced to a seasoned attorney (or agent) who can manage this one agreement on your behalf. Anything beyond that is just a bonus.

IT'S IN THE DETAILS

Other than their eye for detail and basic legal training, there are other values an attorney brings to your table. This may be true for your agent to a large extent, but a good attorney spends all day every day negotiating, talking with business affairs departments, producers, network and studio executives. They know the deal-making culture and the specific terms they can or cannot achieve – all of which varies from one studio to the next, from one producer to the next. Attorneys are also trained to see what's *not* there, what's missing from a deal memo.

Some agents are also gifted in this way, but if an agent is in a hurry, or they're inexperienced as a negotiator, they could miss details or strategic language that is not there simply because it's not in the production company's interest to offer it up front.

In my personal experience, there can be a significant difference between having your deal drafted by or reviewed by an attorney versus an agent. Either way, you want someone who's not merely looking at the topline deal points (fees, backend profit participation, etc.) but someone who is also paying attention to the fine print and is a strategic thinker.

So long as your attorney knows how to artfully negotiate and arrive at fair – meaning both sides are equally happy and equally unhappy with the result – you'll be in good shape. Whether an agent or attorney is handling your early deal-making, it's also imperative you've confirmed with them what kinds of deal points are included and what sort of strategies are in play, since these might be important as precedent for your future. Even

THE VALUE OF A PAPER TRAIL

In all dealings with intellectual property, the paper trail is paramount.

Make written records of every discussion, meeting, deal, con-versation, agreement, modification, exchange, disagreement. The documents you create may well mean a lot of money to you down the road, may save embarrassment, may empower your team to remedy problems, may inform a successful strategy.

A full history is worth its weight in gold, and any agent or manager will thank you and be ever more motivated and well-armed on your behalf. Maintain an ongoing and accurate history of your relationships, meetings, submissions, responses, phone contacts, the comments or representations people make to you, and your network in general. This responsibility is not optional. Please, please get in the habit and keep a journal or notebook in your car, by your phone and computer. Download a voice recorder 'app' to your cell phone so you can record your thoughts as you leave a meeting, while it's all fresh in your memory.

This is imperative not because we're focused on the negative, on the possibility of disagreement, but because we assume success and an enduring career and want to have a complete inventory or history of your relationships, projects, meetings, deals and so forth. Our memories are faulty. Our records help each of us and our team navigate a better, faster, more reliable course on our behalf.

if it's not that relevant today, each agreement you negotiate and sign is an opportunity to add one new clause, achieve one new precedent to build on, and/or slip in one non-deal-breaker that could have very positive implications for your next deal.

Finally, a few tips:

Entertainment attorneys either bill hourly (and those who do may ask for a retainer in advance), or be open to working on commission (typically 5%). I've always opted to work with attorneys on a commission basis, partly because it creates a sense of partnership or teamwork and keeps your attorney invested in your outcome; and partly because it's economically advantageous not to spend thousands of dollars early on.

If both are available, have both an agent and an attorney review your deals; whether an agent is involved or not, I encourage you to have an attorney do the drafting or, more typically, be the one to respond in detail to the deal memo drafted by the other side. If an attorney is not available and an agent is, simply ask them to handle that piece for you.

SOME RULES ARE <u>NOT</u> MEANT TO BE BROKEN!

Ok, so back to rules: you hereby swear a blood oath you will never represent yourself... *AND*... you will never endanger the integrity of your intellectual property by allowing any business to go forward based solely on an oral agreement... *AND*... you will not work for free except in rare cases and only if the terms of that work are well-documented by a writing.

Any time you agree to anything that involves activity relating to your screenplays (or underlying source material that you control, or any other form of intellectual property) everything must be committed to writing. In some cases, a simple confirming email will suffice. In most cases, a slightly more formal memo or agreement will need to be drafted and signed.

It is your right and obligation to never devalue or compromise your intellectual property, let alone your career or income opportunities.

DO AS I SAY, NOT AS I DID

Let me share a cautionary tale, beginning with brief backstory...

*Once upon a time....*The president of production at Warner Bros. phoned me on the heels of the success of our film *Under Siege*, wanting me to help find a screenplay from which we could fashion a sequel. It so happened I'd already sold an action film to Warner Bros that was in development and that could easily be adapted to become the sequel to *Under Siege*. It was titled *In Dark Territory* and was written by Richard Hatem and Matt Reeves, two writers who'd not previously sold a screenplay, and were yet to be produced.

Before I set up their project at Warners, their agent had shopped their script *In Dark Territory* and every company in town had passed on the project. The attorney representing the writers phoned to ask if I'd read it. I did and because the writers were willing to make modest changes, I agreed to market it, despite the fact it had just been turned down by every major studio and quality independent company. I had them change the title and 90 days later I successfully sold it on their behalf to Warner Bros. The writers got their first sale and a check for $250,000. Not bad. And the script got produced, so Richard and Matt were now paid AND produced screenwriters.

Cut to… Richard was no longer working as a team with Matt, but had written the screenplay titled *The Mothman Prophecies*. Despite Richard initially asking me to read it and apparently wanting me to be his producer, his still-agent nixed that idea, apparently sensing a bigger opportunity for himself and/or his client. So the agent shopped the script through a variety of other producers, each apparently chosen for their clout because they had a deal at one of the major studios. Long story short, he failed to get even one offer. The project was passed on by every buyer in town, both studio and independent… except one. So when the agent phoned me to suggest maybe I'd like to have a whack at succeeding where he'd failed yet again (he used different words), I agreed.

I agreed in large part because I'd learned that the one remaining company that had not yet seen the project was a company I liked and respected. The agent intentionally overlooked that company not because it was in his client's best interest to skip over them, but because he had a personal feud with one of the company's executives at that moment in time. I turned that to my advantage and to the advantage of his client.

But here's where I fell from grace. I agreed and in fact submitted Richard's screenplay to this company, based on a verbal agreement with the agent. The agreement was simple: should I prevail, the agent agreed to refrain from closing any literary rights deal with the company on his client's behalf unless and until the terms of my producer deal were confirmed in writing. Since I agreed that this agent would receive a commission on my producing fee, I felt it reasonable to rely on a verbal handshake. His agency would benefit from doing the right thing, and hurt themselves (and me in the bargain) if they went back on their promise. For reasons I can only guess at, the agent was not true to his word, and I learned that the he had closed the writer's deal before my deal was outlined. The result: my fee was instantly reduced by $250,000. Neither the agent nor the owners of the agency could offer any explanation for their behavior.

I won't bore you with other war stories. Suffice it to say when I advocate, better yet insist, that every interaction along your Hollywood career path is documented and signed, I know the cost of ignoring that rule. In just the one example above, it cost me $250,000 in cash income. There were other costs as well, in terms of relationships and aggravation. All this could easily have been avoided. And for your sake, I hope you never experience this sort of thing personally.

The point is simple: the choices and behaviors of one agent (supported by his client) were entirely illogical, irrational, not even self-serving or gaining any form of advantage, economic or otherwise. It simply made no sense at all. In fact, this agent and the agency lost a $50,000 commission from me! Why would someone cut off their own nose? Was it to punish me for succeeding twice where their agent had failed? Did this individual simply lack integrity? No idea, but that's my point. You cannot possibly imagine or predict all the twists and turns as you and your projects navigate the path to ultimate success in Hollywood. You can only trust there will be surprises, and left-turns.

And that's why agreements are so essential to your well-being. People behave better, you preserve healthy relations, your success network expands, your income is more protected and likely. Would the outcome have been different had I insisted on a written agreement? Absolutely yes!

The good news is that these sorts of missteps can be avoided altogether by having a simple signed agreement — holding fast to Rule # 1.

RELEASES

People who don't know you often want or will only accept your script if it's submitted to them by an agent or manager or attorney. The reason is simple.

In a business where all underlying value is predicated on intellectual property, on specific ideas, characters, story and how those are expressed – i.e. copyrighted works - there's the constant threat someone might claim a success was stolen or lifted from their original work. Access to your work therefore comes with a perceived price tag.

If a producer or studio or financier or director agrees to read your work and then passes on it, you could at some future time file a lawsuit if they should finance, produce and distribute or otherwise be associated with a project that bears some resemblance. It all hinges on the legal notion of 'implied contract' – i.e. if a work is produced similar to yours and you weren't paid (AND the production company or someone else associated with that film previously had access to your work – access being the key), you have the right to sue, whether you prevail or not.

As one example, a writer years ago submitted a treatment to Disney and the studio passed. Disney later produced *Honey I Blew Up the Kid*, and the writer of the treatment won a lawsuit because the jury believed the writer's idea had been used (i.e., they believe his copyright work had been infringed).

Lawsuits are time-consuming, annoying, expensive, and not uncommon. I've been named in lawsuits as a defendant, along with the studio and others, on more than one occasion. It usually occurs when a film enjoys economic success at the box office. These lawsuits often turn out to be without merit, as was the case with Pretty Woman and the original Under Siege, but they must be addressed. The desire to avoid these time-consuming problems is what gives rise to the standard industry solution, which is either to refuse to accept submissions directly from writers, or to have writers sign a 'release' before accepting their work.

Your solution to the foregoing:

> (a) create lots of relationships;
>
> (b) get an agent and/or manager;
>
> (c) target companies who accept unsolicited material; and/or
>
> (d) sign releases when requested as a pre-condition to having your script read.

Relationships trump everything else and will smooth the way to being consistently welcomed and having your work reviewed. A reputable agent or manager will also safeguard you and the persons and companies reviewing your work from unmeritorious lawsuits.

THE MORAL...

Don't do as I did, do as I do today and as I preach here. I promise it's best not to spend years trying to undo a problem and, in the arena of intellectual property, some problems can take years if you're lucky.

AVOID THE SCREENPLAY GRAVEYARD

Many a project has simply died a premature death because of innocent, naïve or trusting judgments and decisions – where the writer just couldn't imagine or anticipate the potholes, the quicksand, the intentions or agendas, the choices or behaviors of others.

You want to avoid the heartbreak of mucking up the rights, your project's chain of title or anything that could literally bury your intellectual property or make it legally, and thus commercially, not viable. Any dispute has the potential to ward off any who might otherwise be interested, as if your script were a leper. The mere threat of legal action or other messy wicked problem relating to the health of your IP rights is to be avoided at all costs.

I've beaten this creature until it's dead, but if you leave this session with only one thing imprinted on your conscious and subconscious mind – and that one thing is you promise yourself never to enter into an oral or unsigned agreement, or have your scripts in any sense compromised, I will have delivered sufficient value to sleep well at night.

CREATIVE 'CONTRIBUTIONS' BY OTHERS

Let's go back to some of those phone calls you received just as we were starting this chapter. Take the one from Walter Wannabee first, and let's review what's at stake if you incorporate his creative notes into your script.

When you include in your screenplay any material (idea, dialogue, character, scene, etc.) suggested by someone else, you will not own that material unless it was specifically agreed to in advance. And do I need to add again that the agreement needs to be *in writing*?

If you are going to perform work and spend time to create a new draft that embraces other people's ideas or input, be aware that without a specific agreement to the contrary, that person or persons will actually have an ownership interest in your project, a legitimate claim for their contributed IP. And the problem usually expresses itself in a demand for payment or some percentage of the proceeds of an option or sale of the work, possibly even future profits. To avoid this classic problem, you must arrive at an agreed upon understanding before you commit to or actually do any writing that includes third party ideas.

And the time to agree is BEFORE you begin doing the work. You may have one or more meetings or conversations, but before you boot up your computer and begin to revise your script, that's the moment. BEFORE is natural, easier, a good test of the relationship and everyone's intention. AFTER almost always poses significant problems and disagreements. It's just human nature. So please handle these conversations early on, and have your understanding reduced to a writing that is signed by both parties.

THE CARROT -- aka THE DEAL CONDITIONED ON A REWRITE

Let's go back to that call from Walter Wannabee for a moment. Remember the one where his boss was looking to option your script provided you do a revision and provided you include his notes? Be aware there are two elements here: the revision itself and the ownership of the IP his notes have added to your script.

If a producer asks you to deliver a rewrite (incorporating some of their ideas) before they'll formally option your script, one approach is for you to own the new material outright if they don't trigger the deal within X number of days of delivery of the rewrite (e.g. 30-60-90 days max). If they fail to sign a deal memo and pay you option or purchase money (the terms of which are pre-agreed upon), you own the material outright. *Nothing should ever be left up to good faith negotiations.* You will not be happy with the result. With an agreement signed at the outset, if they don't option or buy your script, you haven't wasted time or effort because you like the changes or added material AND you now are the sole owner of that intellectual property. Of course the deal memo should also protect you as the sole owner of your work even if an option is executed.

Whether the material or ideas are being contributed by a friend or a seasoned producer, you must protect your script and maintain clean chain of title. A sound approach or solution is to agree that, if they don't option or purchase the project by a specified date, you have the right to pay One Dollar in exchange for them assigning their material to you (and that assignment is also signed in advance), so you retain 100% undisputed authorship.

Alternatively, you can assign a value to that material in advance that is fair, so if that other person is not involved in your project going forward, you know precisely what is required, and what dollar amount will protect the integrity of your project. If people are unwilling to agree up front, then the solution is simple: **under no circumstance should you include their ideas or material.**

Trust, but verify.

~ Ronald Reagan

BE TRUSTING, BUT HAVE A SIGNED MEMO TO SUPPORT YOUR TRUST

Your judgment and intuition should guide you in all instances. Take into consideration the quality or experience of the producer, the quality of their notes and ideas, their openness in communicating their plan or intention, if they respond clearly and are they amenable to signing an agreement? The more you can say 'yes' to these questions, the more likely you'll have a successful relationship and result. Either way, make certain you retain control and protect your ownership of the rights in and to your work, unless and until a compelling option or purchase agreement – vetted by an attorney – is put squarely in front of you.

The absence of a clear, written understanding should be a red flag. Memories and agendas and interests can and often do diverge over time, increasing the opportunity for people to make a claim and thus tie up your screenplay. Should there be a dispute of any kind, it reduces the likelihood any other producer will want or be able to actually option your work in the future.

SCRIPT OPTIONS AND AGREEMENTS

Remember back when Isabella at IndieProd called and she just **loved** your script. The only thing was, IndieProd will need a six month free option to make anything happen.

What to do? Is it a foot in the door or a slap in the face? The answer: that depends…

The value of a script option usually depends on several factors.

- Who's optioning it?
- Is it a major studio or an independent?
- How deep are their pockets?
- Is it a producer with a successful track record (whether for studio or independent films)?

Value is not just a dollar-based assessment. If offered the exact same number of dollars for a one-year option on your latest screenplay, *Mr. Blockbuster,* from two different producers, how would you weigh the merits of those competing offers?

Would it matter to you that one offer came from Larry Loser who's intensely disliked around town and has never gotten a single film financed, packaged or produced, and the other offer was from Ms. Former Studio Head Turned Big Time Producer?

What non-economic value is involved in this equation? The answer: nothing short of the future trajectory of your entire career, a relationship of immensely greater currency, a much greater likelihood of your film actually getting produced and onto the big screen, the opportunity to network out from that experience to vastly increase the number and quality of your professional relationships and, finally, the opportunity to negotiate better deal terms since Ms. Former Studio Head is known to produce only large-budget studio-released films.

Even if the dollar amount being offered is truly impressive, be it to option or purchase your project, these other considerations can have tremendously different outcomes and implications for your larger career trajectory.

Options: Nuts And Bolts And Numbers

Have you, as a writer, been previously optioned, sold, or produced? For the first-time writer, there is no set floor or ceiling, no pre-determined fairness formula for the economic or non-economic terms of an option agreement. Very little is 'standard' and deals will vary from project to project. Even after you've been optioned or sold, future deals will still vary and each must be constructed based on the unique circumstances of and the people involved in that deal – yet, you will be setting a precedent or floor for subsequent option agreements.

Market conditions will affect the amount of negotiating leverage you enjoy in any given negotiation.

- How hot is your script?
- Is there competition, or interest from a multiple of productions companies and, if so, how badly do they want it?
- Do you have a name actor or director attached that drives up the value of your project?

There can be any number of factors that affect the real and perceived value of a script in the marketplace.

It's imperative that every option agreement is well-drafted, with all relevant terms agreed upon in advance and committed to paper, and signed *before* the project is marketed to financiers, distributors, agencies or talent… and certainly *before* you render any additional writing services.

It's essential as well that a written agreement not only addresses the terms of the option itself, but spells out precisely every term in the event that option is exercised. In other words, don't simply agree to option your script for a specific number of dollars for one year, and leave everything else to be decided at a later date. Avoid the dreaded phrase "to be negotiated in good faith". *Never ever ever enter into any agreement where essential terms are left "to be negotiated in good faith".* That's an invitation to disaster, because when things get real we often see the lesser side of human nature step to the fore, meaning good

THINKING CREATIVELY ABOUT OPTIONS

Occasionally, you may come across a producer or production company you like, but they lack experience or only have one or two specific quality doors they can open for you and your project.

While this producer or company may not be the one to truly get your project off the ground – or to whom you want to grant a long-term option – there's a way to create a win-win that can benefit all concerned. You can, for example, offer some sort of credit (e.g. associate producer) and a modest fee should they succeed in attaching an important name or element, or any other innovative approach both parties deem fair.

You can then allow that younger producer to submit your project to a pre-agreed short list of names with whom they do have solid relationships (a) on a non-exclusive basis, (b) within a stated time frame, (c) with the understanding you've no further obligation to them, and (d) they've no right during or after the term to shop your project to any individuals or companies not named on the list.

All this can easily be reduced to a signed writing and, if done via email, make certain to have in your files a returned email confirming the understanding with their e-signature.

This approach rewards all for a success, yet still leaves you free to attract and option your project to a stronger producer or buyer down the road.

faith may have just flown out the window. And it's not always any longer in your control or that of the person with whom you originally made the agreement. Suddenly there are agents, managers, attorneys, executives -- a veritable cast of folks who now have a sudden and keen interest in the outcome. A signed writing in advance that addresses all key terms will serve you very well.

I would have to dedicate an entire teleseminar or course to detail for you all the terms and variables that need be negotiated, drafted and agreed to in an option or option-purchase agreement, and all the ways to approach each of those terms or clauses. This is why it's so important you have a good attorney, or agent, on your team. And that every deal is negotiated in advance and 'papered' properly. Nonetheless, what are the basic categories or areas that need to be considered:

Option Agreement Basics

Price

$1,000 is a common option price, rising to several thousand dollars for films in the $5-$15 million budget range. I've optioned projects for as low as hundreds of dollars and as high as $10,000 (the latter was actually a book by a famous author whose works had been optioned and produced on more than one occasion).

For studio and big budget movies, $5,000-$10,000 options may be more common, where that amount may be "applicable against" the final purchase price, as negotiated by the studio and your attorney. Mind you, not all producers can afford to pay such large cash amounts for an option, so they legitimately offer less with the understanding that if they set your project up at a mini-major or major, you will receive a larger sum at that time.

Term

A one year term is very common for an option, with a possible renewal or option extension period of another year. Sometimes you'll see a shorter initial option period, but longer than 12 months is not acceptable in my view unless you're being paid an unusually high option and you've great confidence in the person optioning it based on their track record. I also prefer not to see more than one renewal period in an agreement.

If your producer hasn't made sufficient progress by the end of an extended or second option period (which likely means by the end of year 2), then it's reasonable they either pay your full purchase price or walk away. Of course, you can always negotiate a third option term at whatever price you choose, but again, if no progress is being made, you might feel you're renting your script for not a lot of money.

Also, that renewal period (the second option period) can either be triggered by (a) a simple payment to you of the appropriate, agreed-upon option fee – generally no less than the original year's option fee – prior to expiration of the initial option; or (b) you may negotiate that the option can only be renewed and the second option payment made IF one or more performance criteria have been satisfied.

Some examples of performance criteria or conditions that must be met prior to renewing your option could include:

- A director has been attached,
- One or more lead actors have been attached,
- Full or partial financing has been secured,
- Distribution has been locked in, or
- A foreign sales agent has signed on.

You can pre-negotiate absolutely any element you deem valuable as a condition of someone being able to renew an option on your project.

- If the option is not exercised (or better said, when the option lapses) – which means you've not been paid the purchase price, but have only ever received one or more smaller option payments - all rights will and must clearly revert to you; whoever optioned it walks away with no continuing rights of any kind.
- Ideally, your agreement will include language that explicitly states any writing services you rendered during the option period to further develop the project (based on the producer's input or otherwise) will be owned by you in exchange for payment by you of $1 or more to the producer (or whoever optioned it). In other words, they agree to assign all right, title and interest in any added material so you are free to use that going forward in future versions of your script and future deals. So even before the option lapses, you already have a signed document in your files – an assignment of rights – and all you have to do is pay the pre-agreed amount to make that assignment valid and binding.
- However, if you were being paid for any polishes or revisions you perform during the option period, that might lead to a different arrangement.

- You'll want to know and put in your agreement exactly how many writing steps the producer is allowed to require of you during the option period and how much you will be paid for each step; and, if you are being paid for new drafts during the option/development phase, the cost or "buyback" price of the material may well include some portion of the dollar amounts you were paid to write during that now-expired option period.

Whatever the amount or formula, I strongly encourage you to always have your attorney negotiate terms upfront that secure your right to use all material you write, regardless of whose ideas were involved, regardless of whether you were paid for those changes, whether revisions occurred during an option or not. Always keep control or be able to reasonably buy back control of everything you write.

If, however, your screenplay is being purchased outright (not merely being optioned), then you'll simply want to negotiate and have reflected in your agreement the number of steps and dollars for your performance of any and all 'additional writing services'.

If the purchase is the result of an option being exercised, your agreement will have set out all the essential terms for the acquisition or purchase of your script, including:

- Purchase price: price will likely depend on the scope or budget of the film
- How much if any further writing services or steps are included

Finally, when a producer or a studio makes provision in an agreement for you to perform additional writing steps (e.g. revisions and/or polishes), your attorney or agent will have to define and safeguard you around the issue of what constitutes 'delivery'. A producer or studio will often try to cajole or charm as many free rewrites or polishes out of a writer as possible.

It's fairly standard to ask for some additional work before it's deemed you've officially 'delivered' a particular revision or polish per your contract. It often makes sense or is to everyone's advantage. At some point, however, especially with newer writers, it can cross the line and become abusive. This is where your representatives can really step in and protect you, without you being the bad guy.

Favored Nations Clauses

In option agreements and in purchase agreements, you'll often hear the phrase 'favored nations', which simply means you will be accorded treatment no less favorable than whoever you are 'attaching' to (e.g. if you enjoy favored nations treatment with the producer relative to your definition of profits for the film, then your definition may include a floor, but state that if the producer's deal achieves a better definition, that better definition will apply to you and supersede the lesser definition in your signed agreement).

Favored nations is a negotiating and contractual strategy I like a lot, because it tends to achieve a very fair result while greatly simplifying the negotiation process.

For example, I like to see a writer accorded favored nations treatment with the film's producer in a variety of areas, including:

- Credits (writing, possibly also co-producing etc.), which insures your credit will appear in the same size and type, as well as enjoy the same placement (on-screen or in ads etc.) as the producer.
- Backend or profit participation (i.e. same definition, not necessarily the same percentage); it's realistic, however, to assume first-time writers will receive a percentage, rarely greater than 5%, of the "net" profits, even if the producer, director or talent are receiving a better definition. There's limitless possible definitions for the calculus of backend profits, and the idea is to simply tie yourself to someone with more leverage and negotiating power. Even if you have to compromise and take 2.5% or less of a better definition, you will likely be far better off (5% of 'net' is often not as good as 2% of 'adjusted gross'). Be flexible, innovative, and have that conversation with your attorney or other representative.
- Bonuses (if any): not easy for first-time writers but worth a conversation with your attorney; only likely early on if there's intense interest and competition for your project.

CREATIVE CONTROL – THE MISUNDERSTOOD WHITE ELEPHANT

Even before you ask, the answer to the question is: creative rights are what you do NOT have.

It would be naïve at best to harbor any illusions about maintaining control of your project, your screenplay, or your vision once you've sold it. You simply will not enjoy creative rights or control.

You do, however, have the ability to attract and select a quality producer who will fight for you and protect you to the greatest extent possible. But that's it.

When you sell your home, you give up your right to decorate that house or tell the new buyer how to live in it.

If meaningful creative control is where you draw the line in the sand, then your only practical solution is to raise investor capital, finance the film yourself and shoot your film independently. That's the only time you *may* retain creative control. Even then, you will have to address the needs and concerns of your investors, distributors and others.

A WORD ABOUT WRITING PARTNERSHIPS

Two writers coming together to form a team can often give rise to brilliant collaborations and screenplays, and become the stuff of great and enduring success. Anything is possible when compatible talents and temperaments come together.

By the same token, writing partnerships can pose very real challenges – not necessarily in the writing process per se, but more typically on the business side of the relationship. Every collaboration begins with enthusiasm, optimism, and a creative spark – the big bang moment.

All too often, however, writers inspired to team up dive in headfirst without planning out their relationship, without pausing to consider the business of being partners. Being part of a writing team is a choice with significant implications, and it's a choice that should not be made casually. No different than if you were in any other business, where you'd discuss and understand your responsibilities and obligations in advance, and memorialize them in a partnership agreement.

Conflicts or problems tend to arise only after a screenplay's been completed, usually the result of writers having neglected to fully discuss, let alone create a memo or agreement that outlines their expectations, understanding or rights.

Be open in your conversation and communication, be aware you and your writing partner may be harboring different expectations, or simply haven't considered the kinds of decisions or issues that may lay ahead.

QUESTIONS TO ASK BEFORE ENTERING INTO A

WRITING PARTNERSHIP

What's important to each of you?

What if you reach an impasse regarding the terms of an option being offered?

What if one writer wants to sell their script and the other doesn't? This could be because one decides they want to produce it, or wants to attach as director and the prospective buyer is opposed, or the price or other term or terms satisfies one but not the other member of the team.

What if one likes producer X and the other likes producer Y?

Who's on each of your teams? And who would you agree should spearhead the marketing of your script? Writer A's manager or Writer B's agent or attorney?

If neither has an agent or attorney and you disagree on who you like after taking some meetings, how will you arrive at an agreement?

If you're not mutually satisfied with the initial deal-making process, whose attorney or agent will negotiate any future deals if the partnership continues? If a change needs to be made come the next opportunity, how will you arrive at an agreement?

How many hours each week will you write?

Will you write physically together or separate?

Will you write different scenes and then trade or write the whole of it together?

Are you pooling efforts and not counting who wrote how many pages?

Are you committing to scheduling regular hours each week until the script is finished?

If you go into pitch meetings, how will you pitch as a team? Who will take the lead, or open up the pitch? Who's better in the room?

What happens to the other partner if one becomes unable to write?

Who enjoys what rights vis-à-vis the screenplay and what decision-making role in general will each enjoy?

Is this an ongoing collaboration, or just a one-off partnership?

Is this an equal (50-50) partnership, both in terms of contribution and reward? If you're new and you collaborate with a successful writer, then that would be great for you, but what about that other writer? How will he or she gain value through collaborating with you? What do you gain by collaborating with them?

What are some possible solutions or approaches?

Share your expectations fully, openly and honestly before you begin writing. Invest the time, ask the others' needs, goals, intentions and expectations.

Have an attorney memorialize your understanding in a written agreement, so there's no opportunity for misunderstanding later on.

A collaboration agreement merely needs reflect with full transparency what each expects and agrees will be the dynamic of the partnership. This may change in time, or morph from one project to the next. Be innovative where need be. It could involve a "story by" credit for one, or an unequal split of fees, or some other acknowledgement of whatever is deemed fair.

It tends to become more complicated when your script is finished and ready to be marketed, when more voices get involved in the conversation, including agents, managers, attorneys. And that can lead to an impasse for your project. What seems all sunshine at the outset, I've often witnessed turn into a stream of tension and dispute. When that happens, it's not uncommon to hear "it was my original story" or "I found the idea", or "I did most of the writing" or "I, something"… and the "right vs. wrong" of a relationship can rear its ugly head, where all parties later want to unsheathe their dull, rusty butcher knives.

Investing a little time and conversation, memorializing the business understanding of your relationship, will avoid 99.9% of all potential problems; not that problems or questions or concerns won't arise down the road, but you'll have a roadmap and an agreement, and have established a working 'culture' for your partnership.

And never over-ride your intuition. If you don't think you could, or should, work with a particular writer, then don't. No matter how sweet the deal or the upside may seem. Be thoughtful and take care not to saddle yourself with a person who's a problem even before you go out on a first date. How will you know? By asking one handful of simple questions, by openly assessing their willingness and desire to approach your collective business in a professional manner and address the business of your partnership. If they resist, you might well anticipate that same response or worse when a real issue comes up.

Go with your gut. If you're uncertain, then walk away. If you feel that if you walked away then you'd regret it and feel deeply remiss, then don't. But don't go in wearing a blindfold. Set some ground rules when the bloom is still on the rose. You'll likely avoid problems if you do, and invite them into your life later if you don't.

COPYRIGHT AND WGA REGISTRATION

We've covered the Get Smart and Get Legal portions of the chapter. Now it's time to Get Protected. And you get that protection through copyright registration and registering your script with the Writer's Guild.

Copyright is simple, inexpensive and essential. Copyright registration safeguards the integrity and value of your original content (intellectual property) and forms a solid foundation for you to build a body of work that can be exploited indefinitely, not merely in its original form but across a wide range of media as you adapt and repurpose it in various formats.

It's a great idea to copyright each original work (including new drafts of pre-existing works).

Authors of original works – whether published or unpublished – are entitled to protection under U.S. law and are given the exclusive right to:

- Reproduce the work in copies or phonorecords
- Prepare derivative works based on the work
- Distribute the work to the public by sale or other transfer (rental, lease, lending)
- Perform the work publicly (e.g. musical, audiovisual, choreography etc.)
- Display the work publicly

A legal formality creating a public record of the basic facts of a particular copyright, registration is technically not a pre-condition for protection. However, there are compelling advantages to perfect a registration for your copyrights, including:

- Registration is required as a pre-condition to filing a lawsuit for infringement of copyright.
- So long as registration occurs within 3 months following publication of a work (or prior to an infringement of that work), statutory damages and attorney's fees are available to the copyright owner

who successfully proves infringement in a court of law. Otherwise, only actual damages and profits will be available.

- If made before or within 5 years of publication, registration automatically establishes 'prima facie' evidence in court of the validity of the copyright and of the facts stated in the certificate.
- Registration allows a copyright owner to record the registration with the U. S. Customs Service for protection against the importation of infringing copies.
- Registration may be made at any time within the life of the copyright. Unlike the law before 1978, when a work has been registered in unpublished form, it is not necessary to make another registration when the work becomes published, although the copyright owner may register the published edition, if desired.

REGISTRATION IS SIMPLE AND INEXPENSIVE:

WGA AND COPYRIGHT OFFICE

I recommend you get in the habit of protecting your authorship by registering each work (book, teleplay, screenplay, new versions of any of the foregoing, etc.) with both the WGA and the U.S. Copyright Office.

You can register your work with the Writers Guild of America at their website (*wga.org*) by clicking on the link that says "Register Your Script". You will be given a choice to register online or by mail. I recommend the convenience, instant protection, and gratification of registering online, which currently costs $10 per script for members in good standing of the Writers Guild, or $20 for non-members. It takes very little time and money, but the peace of mind is invaluable.

You can also register your original works with the U.S. Copyright Office and the cost of online registration (electronic filing) is currently $35 per work, while paper filing (which yields a hard-copy registration form) currently costs $50. All of the various forms for original registration, whether for text, images, video, recordings or otherwise, are available on the website for the U.S. Copyright Office (*www.copyright.gov*), as well as their address and phone contact information.

The U.S. Copyright Office website offers an option for electronic filing on its website. It's simple, quick, slightly less expensive, and eliminates the need for copying, duplicating or mailing.

If physically mailing your original work(s) with physical forms filled out and enclosed, please make certain you submit all three elements together – as one complete package – including: application form, filing fee and non-returnable copy of the 'work' itself. You must send all three required elements together at the same time, in the same package. If submitted separately (e.g. the form is mailed in separate envelope), your efforts to protect your work and effect valid copyrights will likely fail, since the U.S. Copyright Office will assume no responsibility for trying to match required elements (original work or intellectual property, form, payment). Unless the elements are submitted together, the U.S. Copyright Office will not process your application, and will likely return your mailed elements and you will have to begin the application process once again.

For most applications, two complete copies of the work are required and it is advisable to always include two as a matter of course. For your particular application and work, please consult a professional or, at a minimum, read the applicable requirements for application available on the Copyright Office website.

EFFECTIVE DATE OF REGISTRATION

Copyright registration will be effective as of the date your materials are received, regardless of how long before you receive a certificate of registration by mail.

Since over 600,000 applications are filed annually, you will not receive an acknowledgement your application has been received. Therefore, if you are mailing your materials (rather than making online application), it is best to send by 'registered' or 'certified' mail and request a return receipt for your records.

LENGTH OF PROTECTION

Original copyright protection today generally endures for the author's life plus an additional 70 years after the author's death.

INTERNATIONAL COPYRIGHT PROTECTION

There is no such thing as "international copyright".

The United States has copyright 'relations' with many countries throughout the world, and as a result, we generally honor each other's citizens' copyrights. However, protection against unauthorized use in any country outside the U.S. will depend on the laws of that particular country or the specific agreements between the U.S. and a particular given country.

Since the United States does not have such copyright relationships with every country, it is advisable to check a listing of countries and the nature of their copyright relations with the United States. To do so, please see Circular 38a, International Copyright Relations of the United States.

WHAT YOU CAN PROTECT

Here's a partial list of what you can protect with copyright:

Literary Works, e.g.:
Stageplay or Teleplay
Screenplays or Treatments
Fiction
Non-fiction
Manuscripts
Musical Works (including accompanying lyrics)
Dramatic Works (including accompanying music)
Pantomimes and Choreography
Motion Pictures (and other audiovisual works)
Sound Recordings

Essentially, if a work is reduced to text, recording, video or film, or other tangible form, you can protect it.

WHAT YOU CANNOT PROTECT...

- Works not "fixed in a tangible form of expression" (not notated or recorded, or speeches/performances not written or recorded)
- Titles, names, phrases, slogans, symbols, designs, lettering, coloring, listings of ingredients or contents
- Ideas, procedures, methods, systems, concepts, etc. (as opposed to a description, explanation or illustration)
- Works with no original authorship (e.g. standard calendars or information taken from public documents or common sources)

COPYRIGHT NOTICES

Different from filing for copyright protection, placing a "notice" on your work is also important. For sound recordings, the notice would include the letter 'P' in a circle, followed by the year and the name of the copyright owner. For all other types of work, the notice would use the letter 'C' in a circle, followed by the year and name of the copyright owner, e.g. © 2012 John Doe. Be consistent and display your name identically in all notices and registrations of your work (e.g. if you use a middle initial, do so consistently).

The notice should be prominently placed on the first page, on the container or other location that gives the public reasonable notice of your copyright claim.

You should place a notice on all your works, whether published or unpublished, as well as on all subsequent revisions, editions or publications.

Place a 'notice' of copyright (e.g. © 2012 Gary W. Goldstein) on your cover or title page or other prominent and readily visible location so the public cannot make a claim your 'notice' was not easily viewed.

Create a habit of including copyright notices on every original work and every version or draft of that work.

Place both the copyright notice and the WGA registration number (e.g. Registered WGA West # 1234567890) at the bottom left corner of your title page.

So that's it – a detailed look at the steps needed to get legal and get yourself protected. Take responsibility for yourself, your intellectual property, and your own career. You'll be glad you did.

MILESTONES

- First Rule: Never agree to anything that is not reduced to a writing AND signed by both parties; this rule is iron-clad vis-à-vis any work relating to your own intellectual property (scripts 'plus') or any work you would perform on someone else's projects/scripts.
- Second Rule: Never work for free, unless there are extreme and compelling reasons, AND you've observed Rule # 1 (the terms and conditions of that work are spelled out in a signed writing)
- Third Rule: Never ever speak business on your own behalf – get an attorney, agent or manager to speak on your behalf (even if they will not be your full-time representative going forward).

- When any circumstance or opportunity suggests a written memo is in order, immediately call your attorney or your agent and, if you have none, use that opportunity to cast your net, seek referrals, and make contact by phone or in person with as many qualified agents and attorneys as possible until you find one you respect and who's willing to help (i.e. represent) you in that moment.
- Always maintain a 'paper trail' to benefit you, your career, current or future representatives, and avoid loss of intellectual property and/or income, embarrassment. Keeping a written history of every discussion, meeting, deal, conversation, agreement or modification of an agreement, disagreements and the like will refresh memories, resolve problems, facilitate strategies.
- Protect your hard work and intellectual property by filing for copyright protection, as well as registering your works with the Writers Guild of America. It's inexpensive, can be done online quickly, and is recommended for every draft of every project.
- Copyright notices: Also remember to include a copyright notice on the title page of each work (e.g. ©2012 Gary W. Goldstein).

We've made our way through the building blocks. Now it's time to get to the fun stuff. You're a storyteller, so that means you have stories to tell.

Next we'll identify your most powerful one.

SUCCESS STRATEGY SEVEN: IDENTIFYING YOUR MOST POWERFUL STORY

Somewhere in your career, your work changes. It becomes less anal, less careful and more spontaneous, more to do with the information that your soul carries.

~ Ben Kingsley

REVEAL THYSELF:

Authenticity Is Your Brand!

I originally met a talented writer by the name of Kimberly via Facebook. Before joining my mastermind *Hollywood Confidential*™, Kimberly wrote me the following email:

> *"Being the impatient person that I am, I want to make sure that I'm doing everything possible to continue to move forward to create a writing career. Continuing to learn has always been a focus for me in any career, so it seems to me that it would be the same for writing, but how do I know when it's time to start reaching out to people for help? Also, how do I know I'm on the right track?*
>
> *I strive to write what's interesting to me and hope that it's interesting to others. I'm not even all that concerned with being a 'famous' writer. I just want to wake up every morning knowing that now my career is as a writer, instead*

of being an application specialist the first nine hours of every day, then being a writer in whatever time is left over.

The big thing for new writers seems to be the way of 'indie' films, but in all honesty, I really like action and sci-fi movies and those are what I want to write.

Growing up, my Cinema Paradiso *of sorts was these types of films. They showed me a place where women were strong and respected for their knowledge and power, whether it was something like* Star Trek: The Next Generation *or a martial arts film. It showed me that what's reality for me (growing up in a tiny little town in the midwest) doesn't necessarily have to be the same in the future.*

The reason I bring this up is because a lot of writers seem to be down on this type of movie. Do you feel it's detrimental for me to focus on this type of writing? I don't exclusively write just action or sci-fi, but I'd rather see Kate Beckinsale in Underworld *than in* Much ado About Nothing. *I liked both films but one just speaks to me more than the others.*

I'd like to know what else I can do to continue to move forward. How do I know when I'm ready to reach out to people who could actually give me a chance? Should I focus on writing what's popular in Hollywood instead of what speaks to me?"

Kimberly's note cuts right to the heart of the matter on two fronts. First, when is the right time to begin reaching out in earnest to people who may be able to help you achieve your career goals? Second, what is the better strategy for a professionally younger writer: to write what's 'popular in Hollywood' or 'what speaks to {you}'?

Action or horror may not be the most typical focus for a majority of women screenwriters. So what? The only measure that matters is: if it's your passion, choose it and do it. If other writers, friends, people inside or outside the industry are not supportive, don't allow their limitations to become your limitations or make you question yourself.

Write what you love, write what you know, write what you must, write whatever you're excited about and stirs your passions. Authenticity as an artist is a magical elixir. It's compelling and undeniable. Your stories are and must be the deepest expression of who you are, what you believe, and reflect the world as you see it.

Passion is the thing that will compel people to listen to you, let people see how much you love what you do, and how much your purpose expresses who you are. Writing what you know and love will shine through the pages, ignite your enthusiasm and that of your readers, empower you to be a better writer, a more persuasive advocate and marketer, deliver more engaging pitches, and more rapidly align the right people to support you and your work. Let people feel and sense the fingerprints of your caring on each page and with each conversation.

Merely trying to mimic the marketplace or second-guess the tastes and preferences of either audiences or the decision makers in Hollywood is a formula for frustration. There's no denying someone who's on fire and loves what they do, especially a storyteller in love with their characters and story. If you're committed to more than the craft of writing, and determined to build an enduring career in the film and TV business, then you must commit to being an original, to consistently make choices and write stories that only you can write. Celebrate your 'voice' as an artist, and don't try to fit in to someone else's notion of success.

That's why you're here. Your mission is to tell your powerful stories, connect deeply with your audience, reconnect to your soul's purpose and carve your own path. Even if you aspire to be hired for assignments, your unique gift and perspective and storytelling voice are the only truly reliable way for people to appreciate who you are and be drawn to work with you. It may feel counterintuitive, but marching to your own drummer is your passport to success.

One of my favorite quotes, by George Bernard Shaw, sums it up rather well.

> "This is the true joy in life: Being used for a purpose recognized by yourself as a mighty one, being a force of nature instead of a feverish, selfish little clod of ailments and grievances, complaining that the world will not devote itself to making you happy. I am of the opinion that my life belongs to the whole community and as long as I live, it is my privilege to do for it what I can. It is a sort of splendid torch which I have got hold of for the moment and I want to make it burn as brightly as possible before handing it on to future generations."

Your torch, your light, your distinctive creative talent and 'voice' is a joy and a magic only you can bring forth. The way you burn brightly is to remain true to your inner voice, to your 'DNA' as a creator and write what burns deeply within you, be it comedy or drama. Your stories bring the possible into reality for audiences in a way no other individual writer can duplicate.

If you were a novelist or painter, a sculptor or architect, or a playwright or other form of artist, no doubt others who'd come before you would be your "influences" – those who inspired you - but you'd never think to mimic them per se. You'd bring the full force of your originality, vision, life experience and unique talent to every one of your creations. It should be no different as a writer, producer, actor or director in film and television.

Be the most authentic you imaginable. Call upon the deepest part of yourself, take the deepest cut and tell unique stories that make others sit up and pay attention.

J.F. LAWTON

Pretty Woman was J.F.'s first 'spec' script after we began working together. He'd written half a dozen or so screenplays before and since dropping out of film school. But this new script, originally titled *3000*, was shockingly powerful, moving, and unlike anything I'd read previously.

I believe his success, all that followed, was the direct result of that one story, that one screenplay, so authentic that Hollywood could not resist embracing his talent.

We'd discussed at length certain ideas and criteria for that script before he began writing. His early scripts showed his craft, but none captured his greater talent, none revealed the depth of his gift or a slice of his soul. Jonathan drew deeply from his life, from the colorful part of Hollywood that was his home at the time, from his feelings on the heels of the demise of a significant relationship. His emotional fingerprints were evident on the pages of that script, in the characters and heart of the story. The original was a drama, a tragic and somewhat dark tale. But J.F.'s story and screenplay were so well-structured, boasting beautifully developed characters, that it was not enormously challenging to transform into a comedy once it found its home at Touchstone (Disney).

WRITING WHAT YOU KNOW

When we talk about 'writing what you know', it's not to be taken too literally. But what you know is the DNA that infuses your story with a deeper sense of authenticity. For example, a father's love for his daughter might well be the impetus to write a story as remote or fantastic or fictionalized as *The Professional* and the core relationship between Jean Reno and Natalie Portman. It's your deeper emotional truth, not just a superficial or literal truth, that wins the day. If you've no idea how a young millionaire shark on Wall Street feels, then don't choose to paint a story with that particular brush. Use the brush that is second-nature to you as you hold it in your hand. You can't camouflage emotion, the deeper contours of your characters and their inner world.

J.F. Lawton was neither a prostitute nor a wealthy investment banker, nor was his story about his real-world experience as a freelance computer guy. His story did, however, call upon his emotional experience and his day-to-day reality living in Hollywood, and how he felt about it.

UNDER SIEGE

J.F. Lawton's next spec script was something I encouraged him to write, having learned about his experiences in the Coast Guard Reserve, and the counter-terrorist training he'd received on the eve of the Olympics coming to Los Angeles. As fictionalized as that story was, the world he created was drawn from his personal experience and the unique vernacular he learned during his service. The world he created was infused with his intimate experience serving in the Coast Guard. The quality of writing plus this sense of authenticity is, I believe, why that script not only sold for a significant amount, but quickly found its way into production. It attracted a major studio, star talent, seasoned director, and full cooperation from the Navy because it was such a compellingly authentic read.

Jonathan went on to write screenplays for Joel Silver, Richard Donner, James Cameron and many others. Again, I believe all of those meetings and opportunities flowed from the overwhelmingly consistent response to the story and characters he created in 'Pretty Woman'. These meetings and opportunities cropped up before *Pretty Woman* was released, and certainly before *Under Siege* was in production.

He was able to direct one of his own scripts for Universal, as well as create and executive produce a TV series that ran for four seasons. All this in addition to being hired to write or rewrite numerous projects for A-listers at the studio level. That's the power of one extraordinary script that does not mimic the marketplace but rather is so individual, so compelling, so original that it becomes undeniable. And that's why it's so crucial writers write constantly. It's almost never the first or second or even third script that launches a career in this way. And that's as it should be. It takes a certain amount of experience and writing to be truly prepared to embrace success and move to that next level. No different than any other discipline or industry.

THE MOTHMAN PROPHECIES

Authentic and powerful for entirely different reasons, *The Mothman Prophecies* was based on a true and extraordinarily unusual story. Because the story struck such a deep personal chord for me, the writer and I shared a calling to get this film made.

In a meeting I described in an earlier chapter, it was only partly the story, characters and events within the script that won the day. Confirmed in later conversation with an executive, I was convinced my advocacy, my endless ardor for this story, made all the difference. *Mothman* was a film that could just as easily not have been produced. It wasn't an obvious choice.

The lesson I took away was that it's as important, sometimes more so, to be profoundly and emotionally honest and generous in describing not only the creative merit of your project, but your *why*. Why are you so devoted to telling this particular story, where does your personal passion come from, what compelled you to write it, why do you know in your heart of hearts this material will connect with filmmakers, actors, audiences. I spoke my truth as if it was the closing argument in a life and death trial, and that tipped the scales from a 'pass' to a 'yes'.

As different as each of these three films are from one another, they share in common a quality or foundation of authenticity that helped make them undeniable and powerful.

CHOOSE WISELY, STAY THE COURSE

You choose to become a writer, producer, director, actor or some combination of those talents for a reason. It's not because you crave the risk of freelancing in a globally-desirable and competitive profession. It's because you feel a calling to express yourself in these ways.

Careers in film and TV are launched because an artist demonstrates a 'voice' that is unique, writing and championing stories that stand out and are positively different from the majority. Different in a way that attracts and galvanizes the best of breed in this business. Often it's one script that works the magic. You have to have paid dues, written perhaps a handful of scripts that went unnoticed, and be able to continuously deliver that quality of storytelling that will sustain success once it's yours. But success is a choice. Once you decide and if you truly commit, those early projects are not failures, but stepping stones. They're indispensable and necessary to your process and your future.

AUTHENTICITY 101:

DANCING TO YOUR OWN DRUMMER

Diablo Cody is a screenwriter, writer, blogger, journalist and author. With her avant-garde appearance, asymmetrical haircut and tattoos, and very unique way of doing things, Diablo Cody personified authenticity with her debut screenplay *Juno*, winning an Oscar in 2007 for her efforts. Beyond her Academy Award for Best Original Screenplay, her film received Oscar nominations for Best Directing, Best Picture and Best Actress, as well as winning an Independent Spirit Award for Best Screenplay and a nomination for a Golden Globe, in addition to other awards. This outsized success and audience pleaser, released by Fox Searchlight, ignited a starburst of opportunity.

Cody sold a script (*Girly Style*) later that year to Universal Studios, and a horror script titled *Jennifer's Body* to Fox Atomic, which starred Megan Fox in the lead role.

Cody then created *United States of Tara*, a DreamWorks comedy series starring Toni Collette and produced by Showtime, based on an idea by Steven Spielberg, which ran for three seasons. She was also brought on board to revise the script for the remake of the horror classic *The Evil Dead*.

In December 2011, Paramount released *Young Adult*, starring Charlize Theron, Patrick Wilson, and Patton Oswalt. This was her second collaboration with *Juno*'s director, Jason Reitman. Cody's feature film directorial debut "Paradise" is scheduled for release by Image Entertainment later this year.

Cody gained experience and notice as a blogger, journalist and author. And her first screenplay was so unique, emotionally moving and unusual that it not only got produced and released to great acclaim, but launched a career that successfully spans film and TV.

Not in any sense typical, Cody continues to express her unique storytelling in her blog, not to mention *Red Band Trailer*, the YouTube-based web series she writes, produces and hosts. The latter has thousands of subscribers and her videos have been watched well over 1,000,000 times.

There are many success stories over the last several years, yet hers stands out as a brilliant example of someone who was in no sense typical and who surprised the community with a writing style and decidedly original story that became a *cause célèbre*, launching her career, opening doors, bringing her to the attention of and into relationship with best of breed in Hollywood. No mimicry, no second-guessing, just sheer heart and originality. That was the key for Diablo Cody, and that's the key for you.

AUTHENTICITY 201:

SUCCESS COMES IN MANY SHAPES AND SIZES

One of my favorite success stories was *Half Nelson*, starring Ryan Gosling and Shareeka Epps, a film based on a 19-minute short film made several years earlier titled *Gowanus, Brooklyn*. The film tells the story of an inner-city junior high school teacher with a drug habit who forms an unlikely friendship with one of his students after she discovers his secret.

What's so impressive is that *Gowanus, Brooklyn* was a collaboration between writer Anna Boden and director Ryan Fleck, who teamed again to reprise their short as a feature length film under the new title *Half Nelson*. The film was made without distribution or financial assistance from a major, at a total budget of $700,000. Indie distributor THINKfilm jumped on board after seeing the film screened in competition at the 2006 Sundance Film Festival.

LA Weekly critic Scott Foundas wrote, "At a time when most American movies, studio made or 'independent,' seem ever more divorced from anything approximating actual life experience, *Half Nelson* is so sobering and searingly truthful that watching it feels like being tossed from a calm beach into a raging current."

The film and characters took the audience into a world so believable, so complex and morally ambiguous yet compelling, without attempting to 'clean it up' or resolve these relationships or themes by film's end. In no sense typical, this little $700,000 film won a surprising amount of attention and awards, including an Oscar nomination for Ryan Gosling's performance and a Jury Prize at the Deauville Film Festival.

All this resulted from a writer and a filmmaker who had the moxie to make a short film in the first place. Unlikely though it may seem, it is in fact the formula for success. All successes are built on passion, great story, persistence, and taking imperfect action. Not waiting for permission is one of the most brilliant life strategies for those bold enough, courageous enough to just make things happen for themselves.

To become undeniable, choose to write stories that are unique, authentic, and powerful for you. Write stories that no one else could conceive or write quite the way you can. Let your scripts take people on a journey into worlds and characters you care about deeply and know well. Let your eyes, heart and experience move us through your words and characters. Dare to write what feels risky, however fictional or comedic or dramatic.

WRITE FROM YOUR PASSION

Most people approach their work as if it's something that lives three feet in front of them. We all too often, consciously or unconsciously, build a wall between our work and our personal passions, and it both limits us and deprives others of the full and true measure of our value and genius.

Your motto as a storyteller should be: do your passion, write what you know and care about deeply. Passion is not just about deeply personal emotional stories told as dramas or comedies, but about pursuing that which truly excites you. While you have to be strategic, it's imperative that you be powerful and amazingly truthful.

As Anne Morrow Lindbergh said: 'The most exhausting thing you can do is be inauthentic'. Or another brilliant adage uttered by Field Marshall Ferdinand Foch: 'The most powerful weapon on earth is the human soul on fire'.

Don't settle for being excellent, choose to be amazing.

I've endeavored to sell lots of ideas and projects. Many succeeded, yet many failed. In hindsight, I can share what for me is the lesson learned. Perhaps not a perfect or universal measure, but the project written from a deeper place of emotional truth and or simple passion will outdistance the competition. Whether your early work gets produced or not, one magnificent screenplay can distinguish you and do more for your career than beautifully executed stories that lack your 'DNA'.

OSCAR®

In fact, if we look at films that have garnered nominations and/or wins at the Academy Awards in recent years, many are a-typical of what we historically consider classic candidates for the Academy. Some of the choices are influenced because the public is voting too; and the movie-going public pre-selects (along with some critical response) which films are even in the running when it comes time for the Academy to nominate films. What better measure of what 'works' than audiences and Academy members? Take a look at the following titles that walked off with an Oscar. Note the diversity represented in the list. None are typical "Hollywood" stories. Reflect on the personal passion that brought each to the screen, and be inspired.

- *The King's Speech* (2010) 12 Nominations; 4 Oscars (including Best Original Screenplay)
- *The Fighter* (2010) 7 Nominations (including Best Original Screenplay); 2 Oscars
- *Slumdog Millionaire* (2009) 9 Nominations; 7 Oscars (including Best Adaptation)
- *The Wrestler* (2008) 2 Nominations
- *Milk* (2008) 8 Nominations; 2 Oscars (including Best Original Screenplay)
- *Juno* (2007) 4 Nominations; 1 Oscar (Best Original Screenplay)
- *Little Miss Sunshine* (2006) 4 Nominations; 2 Oscars (including Best Original Screenplay)
- *Letters from Iwo Jima* (2006) 4 Nominations (including Best Original Screenplay); 1 Oscar
- *Crash* (2004) 6 Nominations; 3 Oscars (including Best Original Screenplay)
- *Goodnight, and Good Luck* (2005) 6 Nominations (including Best Original Screenplay)
- *Million Dollar Baby* (2004) 7 Nominations (including Best Adaptation); 4 Oscars
- *Hotel Rwanda* (2004) 3 Nominations (including Best Original Screenplay)

A quick study of the above film titles is enough to make any of us feel proud and excited to be a part of a professional community of storytellers that bring to the world this sort of original, inspired, unique fare.

WHOSE CAREERS DO YOU MOST ADMIRE?

Make a list. Include writers, directors, actors, producers. You'll likely find you admire and appreciate a group of individually unique talents. The ones whose careers you would want to emulate and some of whom will end up on your 'Top 100' list. Study how they began, the choices they've made and see if you discern patterns or ideas for how you want to shape and navigate your career in Hollywood.

I noticed early on some common traits among those I admired. Their early films were not overly ambitious, but entirely original. Baz Luhrman's *Strictly Ballroom*, Mark Waters' *House of Yes*, Steven Soderbergh's *Sex, Lies and Videotape* and so many more. These films were fresh and not overly ambitious. The stories and characters were compelling, and the films were often made on very modest budgets. Even now, Oren Peli's debut film, *Paranormal Activity*, was made for all of *$15,000*.

Can it be done? Absolutely. Is this the only consideration? Absolutely not. But originality wins the day in each instance.

FOLLOW YOUR HEART AND YOUR GUT

It's more than okay to follow your passion, your intuition and your heart. It's the single most reliable success strategy for any creative person. Follow Kimberley's example and identify what's playing in the *Cinema Paradiso* of your mind. Give voice to what you care about most, not what you think others might like. Besides, you can never truly know what others will like.

Success in Hollywood is about the inner game and the outer game. So dare to be different, dare to be exactly who you are and do exactly what you love. Wake up each day excited because you're creating something that is so extraordinary and right for you.

Be no less passionate as a marketer than as a creator. Be as excited and responsible for your career and progress as you are about your writing. Celebrate the opportunity to invest 30 minutes every day being your own best advocate and representative. The more active you become, the more relationships you create, the more it becomes a fun habit, an exhilarating part of your day and the key to creating and sustaining an enduring career as a professional in the film and TV business.

And finally, work at becoming an ever more persuasive oral storyteller. Coach yourself or be coached, take courses, find a teacher or mentor. Be able to persuade people and hold them captive with your stories. Become the greatest possible advocate for your projects and let people know why you were compelled to invest so much of yourself in your stories and scripts.

MILESTONES

- Authenticity is your 'brand'; write what speaks to you as a creator, not what you think might be popular in Hollywood in any given moment. Don't bother trying to second-guess Hollywood or audience appetites or trends. Dare to write what feels risky.
- Writing 'what you know' (literally or otherwise) naturally infuses your story with a greater sense of authenticity.
- Respect your 'voice' and make consistent choices to write the stories that no one else could write quite the way you can; take the 'deeper cut' that makes others sit up and pay attention.
- As a storyteller, fall in love with your characters and story, take people on a journey into worlds and characters you care about deeply and know well, which will only connect you more deeply with your audiences, inside and outside Hollywood.
- While everyone must learn and 'pay dues', it's often one powerful and unique script (commercial or otherwise, comedy or drama), written with unfailing authenticity, that captures the magic and launches an enduring career.
- Be no less passionate about your work as a marketer than as a writer or creator.
- Become the greatest possible advocate for your projects and persuasive teller of stories; get coaching, find a mentor, take courses… be able to hold people captive with your stories AND your passion and confidence.

So seven steps are under your belt: you've mastered the concepts of networking, branding, and developing your D.O. list; you recognize the power of assistants, the importance of building your dream team, and the necessity of getting your work the legal protection it needs. As promised, we're into the fun stuff. Because now that you've identified your most powerful story, you're going to sell it. And this is where you pay special attention to that last paragraph up above, because you're going to sell your story by the way you tell your story

That's what's known as pitching, and that's next.

SUCCESS STRATEGY EIGHT : MAKE EVERY MEETING COUNT

How To Be Extraordinary In The Room

The key to success is to raise your own energy. When you do, people will naturally be attracted to you.

~ Stuart Wilde, author and metaphysician

To be amazing, to raise your energy, to stand out, to excite, captivate and be remembered, to be 'good in a room', is a skill we all must *learn* and *earn*.

Learn because there are techniques and things to be mindful of that come with experience and study, and from repeatedly doing the thing you want to improve at; *earn* because maturity and confidence are the by-products of doing things that initially feel uncomfortable, thus consistently growing the confidence to 'raise your energy'.

The real key is having the confidence to be different, to be you, to tell your story and not worry about pleasing your audience or second-guessing what you think they may be wanting to hear. This goes to the heart of what I talk about elsewhere in this book about being authentic, allowing you to more naturally and deeply connect with and express your value to the people you meet along your journey.

ONE PART MARKETING, TWO PARTS 'SHINE'

A meeting is one part marketing (which may include a pitch) and two parts being the shining personality they'll want to invite back. You're prepared, so comfortable that questions or interruptions can't throw you.

You're ready to engage, keep folks riveted and entertained.

A meeting is so much more than an opportunity to land a job; it's the perfect opportunity to sparkle, to let others come to appreciate you, your story and your talent. Nothing in the human experience is so powerful as that moment of 'bonding'. It's natural, fun, builds instant rapport, and lets other become excited about you. A good meeting opens the door to a future rich with opportunity and introductions. It's never just about whether you're the ideal writer for a given project.

Are you someone they like and feel would be smart, fun and enjoyable as a collaborator? Are you someone who contributes talent <u>and</u> a good energy, a unique persona, making every experience a greater success just for your presence?

> ## WHAT CONSTITUTES A MEETING?
>
> A meeting may be in-person, or any initial interaction.
>
> Think of every phone conversation, general meeting, or written communication as a meeting.
>
> Treat each of these moments with the same amount of thoughtfulness as if you were literally 'in the room'. Consider how you interact with the assistant or any member of their team. Look at every interaction as an opportunity for people to get to know you better. Build human bridges by putting your personality and humanity first, business second.

PITCH

Great stories deserve a great pitch, and you deserve to receive the disproportionate benefits that are the direct and often immediate result of delivering a great pitch.

The 'pitch' has become a time-honored, institutionalized part of the process of setting up any film or TV project in today's Hollywood. Pitches are how we communicate most effectively and economically about the two most valuable currencies in all the film and TV business: brilliantly inspired fresh projects and the talent that birthed them into the world. Both currencies – you, the creative talent, and the new project you're pitching – are equally valuable.

Hollywood thrives on discovering new projects that can strike gold with audiences, investors, distributors, agents, directors, actors and, of course, everyone's bosses (everyone has one). It's the lifeblood of the business in general, essential for the continued growth of any company or individual career, and feeds the seemingly endless appetite for quality entertainment inside and outside of Hollywood.

It seems odd, given the number of screenplays and teleplays registered each and every year with the Writers Guild of America and/or the U.S. Copyright Office, but the reality is there's a perpetual scarcity of quality projects to satisfy the appetites of all the top directors, actors and other talent whose craft and livelihoods depend on a fairly consistent flow of product. Agencies and management firms feel constant pressure to discover and deliver into the hands of their star clientele the caliber of project that will satisfy. Even the largest agencies cannot possibly find enough quality material to effectively service more than the top 25% of their client roster.

RELATIONSHIPS ARE RESULTS

My mantra in life and in Hollywood is: 'Relationships trump results'.

For that reason, I encourage every creative person to pick up the phone, send query letters, submit scripts and short films, set meetings and pitches. Your primary motivation, first and foremost, is to create and broaden and deepen your relationships in the Hollywood community. Strange as it may seem, your goal is not necessarily to sell, option, or get hired. If you sincerely desire an enduring and successful career in film and/or TV, there is no substitute. Getting in the room to pitch, literally or virtually, is the highest and best use of your time, the single most effective means of letting others get to know you both personally and professionally.

By the same token, the pitch is the perfect opportunity for everyone in the business of film and TV to discover that new 'voice' that also happily happens to be the personality that's smart, easy-going, confident, talented and open to new ideas and positive collaboration. It's as important to discover and nurture relationships as it is to find one amazing project. One great relationship will yield many introductions, meetings, referrals, and conversations for years to come. Create a quality network and you'll enjoy a steady stream of opportunities to pitch, to sell, to get on staff, *to be hired*.

WHO CAN YOU PITCH?

Pitches are not the unique province of agents and producers, not by a long shot. Everyone engaged in Hollywood is looking for material. Even cinematographers and editors and casting directors are looking to up their currency by being the one to unearth and deliver into the proper hands a potentially valuable property – and to be attached to should that project move into production. The same is true for everyone.

Who's everyone? Actors, producers, agents, managers, casting directors, story analysts, directors, financiers, distributors, foreign sales agents, independent and studio executives at all levels (from the mailroom to the development exec to the senior vice president of production and right up to the chairman), and the list goes on and on. Even attorneys are on the prowl, one eye peeled for new clients, the other mindful they can earn big brownie points by introducing a page-turner to their best friends in the business and/or to their existing clients. It's hard to think of a population within Hollywood that's not engaged in the eternal quest to discover that next great story.

If you take these ideas to heart, you'll recognize pitch opportunities lie around every corner, with virtually every successful person in the business, and are by no means limited to agents and producers. In fact, the best short cut to quality agents and producers is often to target your pitch to everyone else and, in turn, get referred to agents and producers by people they know, like and trust. Few think to do it, but it's a brilliant strategy that widens your network smartly and rapidly, all the while introducing your latest script to people who matter. For more on this, refer back to the chapter in this book on 'Networking'.

So how and where do pitches take place? Anywhere. They take place in increments from one minute to 15 or 20 minutes. They take place over the phone, in offices, at film festivals or other screenings, at pitch festivals, or simply the result of an unexpected meeting online or at your local coffee shop. Don't be linear in your thinking or marketing. Give yourself permission to color outside the lines and be as innovative as possible. The more quality people who meet you, who hear your pitch, the better. You simply cannot predict who will be the one to refer you to the right producer, to the enthusiastic representative, to the executive who will champion you and your work.

PITCHING IS ONE OF YOUR MOST RELIABLE TOOLS

It's important to become studied and comfortable pitching because it's become more rather than less critical to your success and your project's success. It's a tribal rite of passage, one that you'll come to appreciate both for the ease of in-person relationship building (especially around your mutual love of story and film or TV) and for how a good pitch will dramatically boost your project's chances for getting optioned, purchased, produced or simply to get you called back into more meetings on other, un-related projects.

Nothing says *you* like a pitch meeting. You get to express who you are as an individual and as a talented professional. You sit knee-to-knee in that perfect moment where everyone is focused on you and your story. You have a captive audience that wants you to succeed, wants you to surprise the heck out of them, wants to find in you a brilliant talent and collaborator who's about to deliver into their laps the most undeniably exciting project they could ever imagine.

Writing on spec is one of the top three keys to success, shaving years off your rise to the top, and a brilliant practice that will open more doors than any other single career choice you can make. Yet, even if writing on spec is your habit, and you've one or more completed scripts in hand, you must be prepared to pitch: to *tell* your story in such a way that it *sells* your story. Being able to sit with others and confidently, persuasively, concisely guide others into the heart of your characters and story is the sine qua non of success in Hollywood. It's a grand slam experience that bonds you to them, bonds your listeners to you and your story, arms them with just the right 'pitch' that they can in turn use to create consensus and foster an excitement within their company. Buyers need to see your project's potential and no one is better-equipped than you to foster that vision and enthusiasm and leave them feeling you've conceived a story that will not only connect with audiences, but with financiers, filmmakers and actors.

No money will be handed over, no contracts drafted, until you as the creator have been in the room and they have a sense of you, see you're someone they want to work with, that it will be fun and you're open to their ideas. This is part of what will get communicated behind your back, once you've 'left the room', and they're in staff meetings or on the phone with others they want to attract to your project.

DESIGNING YOUR PITCH

Remember the three basic elements of your logline discussed above:

- **Who** the story is about;
- **What** the character strives for;
- **What** stands in the way.

Your pitch should begin with your logline, then explore those items in greater depth. These plus several other items are the 'must-haves' to maximize the impact from your pitches:

- Begin with your logline to anchor your story and your audience by painting a picture (often referred to as 'baiting the hook'), so your listeners know what movies they're watching in their imagination;
- Focus on the central character that makes your story feel a 'star' vehicle (who the story is about);
- Describe the basic dilemma of the lead character (what the character strives for);
- Describe what's at stake, including any essential conflicts, antagonists or obstacles the lead character must overcome, and how they alter the lead character in some fundamental way (what stands in the way);
- Color in the lead character's emotional-physical-mental state and changes that occur over the course of the story (different from the action of your plot-line);
- Describe the location or environment of the story;
- Unlike your logline, which neither depends on nor needs give away your story's ending, your pitch should conclude with an ending that captures your listeners by surprise, that does justice to your story, is entertaining and audience-satisfying;
- And don't be nervous! Remember, you're with like-minded folks who're excited and want you to succeed, who want to be blown away by you and your story; think of it as a date with someone who you know already wants to go out with you. The worst that can happen is you leave having gained rapport and a growing opportunity for friendship with everyone in that office, including the assistant. It's a win-win-win, regardless of whether your project is a 'fit' for that producer or agent or what-have-you at that particular moment. Assume the odds are modest at best, and you're just there to win over new friends and have fun and enjoy the opportunity to talk about what you love with people who share you creative interests.

As you leave the pitch, your audience's reaction should be:

- Your story is smart, fresh, cast-able, marketable... a perfect opportunity for them!

- Your story is well-crafted, well-paced, without huge gaps in action or logic, and has heart.
- Whether comedy or drama, your story will move audiences; if a comedy, it's undeniably funny; if a thriller, it's suspenseful and offers up surprising twists; if a horror story, it's truly scary; if an action film, it's non-stop excitement, etc.
- Your lead roles will be catnip to actors, and audiences will relate to and love them.

Similar to your logline, albeit in expanded fashion, focus on the core concept and forget about extraneous details, supporting characters unless absolutely necessary to showcase why your lead character behaves a certain way… but best not to describe supporting characters or subplots.

In that same spirit, keep your audience in your story by avoiding any industry vernacular or ideas about how scenes would be shot or any other 'editorial' that breaks the flow of your story and could cause their 'suspension of disbelief' to suddenly come un-suspended.

Avoid any attempt to describe "who" the audience is for your project (if not evident, your pitch may need some tweaking).

Similarly, don't mention your project's budget unless asked, then reply if you have a clear idea based on a budget prepared by a qualified line producer. If not, it's best not to guess or suggest a 'range' of dollars.

Unlike in a query context, be prepared to pitch multiple projects in a live meeting environment: a minimum of one completed script (preferably two that are market-ready), as well as the one or two story ideas you're next planning to write. In other words, be ready for quality meetings and the oft-asked question: what else are you working on?

Finally final: If asked about your professional background or 'credits' and you have none, do NOT be apologetic and do NOT shy away from the question. Answer it straight on in a truthful and humble manner, which just might be "I'm a relatively new screenwriter and haven't yet sold a script or been produced. I've written X number of screenplays (or adaptations or books, etc.), I do (or do not) have an agent and/or manager, and I'm just excited to share my story with you today. So thank you for your time." Assuming you've done your homework and researched not only the company you're visiting, but the individuals you're meeting with as well, you've likely found something you have in common (always good to create a sense of connective tissue) and certainly something that person or company has achieved (e.g. a film they produced that you greatly admire) as the basis for a simple, non-flowery compliment.

PRACTICE MAKES EXCELLENT

Even if you're new to pitching and do not consider yourself a natural at public speaking, or if you're shy or self-conscious (which most are), you can learn to pitch your stories like a pro.

For different pitch environments, you'll want different length pitches for each project, keeping your shortest version under 3 minutes. This might work, for example, at a 'pitch fest'. The shortest version still allows you to get to the essence of your story and emotionally connect your audience to your characters. Let the brevity of your pitch be an asset, prompting conversation and questions. There's strength and confidence in leaving people wanting to know more. You can always go into a longer pitch or more detail if you've so aroused their curiosity that they follow your brief pitch with one or more questions.

Get in the habit of practicing with others different versions (and lengths) of your pitch. Practice delivering it one-on-one, doing it in a room with several people, pitching over the phone. Practice until you feel a sense of ease regardless of how different the environments, the number of people in your audience, how it feels to pitch to different personalities, and whether you're delivering a shorter or longer version of your pitch.

Get as much feedback as you can. Where did the story slow down, where did a listener begin to lose focus or interest, where did your audience become confused? Watch to see where their body language changed for the better or for worse. Take notes and use whatever feedback makes sense and gives you legitimate clues how to improve your storytelling for that particular project.

Practice until you know your pitch so well you can deviate from your rehearsed or 'scripted' pitch, so that if you're interrupted by questions, you won't lose track or feel confused. And remember, if you're blessed to be interrupted by questions, that's a sign you truly have their interest and it's a brilliant opportunity to engage them and sense where they want to know more. Some writers go so far as to practice delivering their pitch backwards, knowing it so well they don't need to memorize or follow a linear script, and no interruption will diminish their ability to put across the best version of their story.

It's crucially important to stay present with the person or people in the room. If it means not remembering each and every line or point you want to make during your pitch, that's alright. People sense when you're reciting versus when you're connecting. They know when it's coming from a place of excitement and passion versus when you're nervous and just moving through your script.

We're all wired to consciously and/or subconsciously know when you're talking with us, not at us. It creates a different energy altogether, a more engaging and embracing energy and mood. Be relaxed, confident and sufficiently practiced so that any question or interruption doesn't throw you.

Practice pitching in front of your video camera, webcam, or in front of friends. Even post your video pitch in a private writer forum for feedback. The more you do, the more it will boost your confidence and improve the effectiveness of your pitch. Encouraging people to give candid feedback to a video pitch can be a powerful learning tool. Seeing yourself on video – for most of us, at least for the non-actor like me – may initially be a horrifying experience. Yet it's the greatest teacher imaginable. Since the camera never lies, we get a profoundly honest sense of our energy, how relaxed we are, how well we're capturing the core or essence of our story, how entertaining we are in our presentation, how effective we are overall.

I try to make it a habit that when I speak in public to always video record my talk. It's been the single greatest motivator for me to learn to quickly grow as a speaker. Every time I do it, I find more ways to improve. Used in tandem with third party feedback, video objectively measures our progress. And, in certain instances, a video pitch itself can become a valuable tool.

If you want to take it up a notch, take an acting class or hire a coach. Pitching aside, learning the craft and challenges faced by actors or producers or others with whom you'll be interacting professionally can only help you empathize, speak their language and give you a far greater appreciation and knowledge of the industry that you now make your home.

Commit to practicing pitching more than is typical for the majority of screenwriters. It will pay huge dividends for you and separate you out from the 97 percent who don't enjoy it, aren't very good at it, don't embrace the opportunity or discipline of becoming better at it.

IT'S NEVER A COMPETITION

Wherever you find yourself, walking into an office, greeting people over a phone line, bumping into someone at a film festival, recognize the happy circumstance and share a bit of yourself and your current project. You see the moment for what it is: a simple opportunity to connect with someone who could be an important friend, and a colleague and collaborator. You see everyone who's passionate and legitimately in the film or TV industry as a possible mentor, teammate, friend, collaborator. So your goal is to connect, to get to know, to let them get to know you and come to an appreciation of your ideas and ability both as a writer and as a storyteller.

You're simply not competing for short-term result and certainly not for dollars. Bring the best of you to each moment, to your writing, to your pitching, to the way you meet people and results will inevitably follow. Dollars will follow. But in the moment, the only competition you're engaged in is to be the very best version of you. Not to impress, but to get better, to be better, to become excellent.

Alfred Hitchcock once said "casting is 65 percent of directing". I'll take that statement and raise it. *Pitching may be 75% of getting hired.* And that's good because it's something that's within your control. Members of the WGA earn far more income from being hired than for selling original scripts. But it's the original spec work and their pitching ability that combine or conspire to get them the paying work that helps sustain a long-term successful career in Hollywood.

A great pitch wins the day, a lesser pitch will not. So practice until you pitch the fullness of your personality and your story every time. The biggest part is not delivering a 'perfect' or flawless or impeccable pitch. The big win is letting others see how deeply you know your characters, how passionate you are about this story, how enthusiastic and positive and open-minded you are, how natural and enjoyable it is to sit in a room with you. So don't trip yourself up should you happen to slip up occasionally in the middle of a pitch. That's not the heart of the matter.

TAKING IT ON THE ROAD

Once you've written, re-written and polished your logline and query letter, and practiced, honed and refined your pitch, there are many quality environments and opportunities to try out your new material and skills. I'll mention just a couple, but urge you to search via Google, look at websites that rate and offer user comments and reviews, and ask people you respect which organizations sponsor worthwhile pitch-fest events. While I cannot endorse any particular festival or organization or event, there are many reputable ones to choose from when looking to get out into the world and try out your new tools, your new pitch. Here are just a couple of examples and you'll find countless more, but the key is to research what other writers have to say on the heels of their experiences.

I've had former students report good experience at FADE IN's Fade In PitchFest, which offers both a 'live' event in Los Angeles and a 'Skype'-based pitch event. For the Skype event, you can have your notes right in front of you. It's a real pitch in real time to real professionals, yet you can have your notes to guide you. The average pitch time is five minutes and you can research each company, see in advance what type of material each company is looking to find. The good news about this and other pitch events is that only those open to and committed to finding new talent and projects show up, so you're assured a receptive audience.

VirtualPitchFest.com is another option for you not only to practice but potentially meet quality people. Their website lists all participating players (what they call 'the pros'), listed by category, e.g. producers, agents and managers. For all participants, you'll find basic information, including company name, recent credits, what they're seeking.

These are only two examples of the opportunities out there. Research where and when you might be able to pitch next and put it prominently on your calendar. I've found that both researching and having an impending deadline on your datebook can be enormously inspiring!

ADVOCACY – a/k/a THE 'OTHER' PITCH

When you are confident enough to engage your pitch audience from your own personal experience – outside the four corners of your storyline or characters – you build a rapport and sense of authenticity that adds a dimension to the pitch experience that makes you stand out. More than that, it makes you memorable.

When you honor your audience by sharing your personal passion, your *why* for writing a particular story, you elevate your meeting to an entirely different experience and quality of connection with people. Tell the 'story behind the story', the reason you were compelled to write this project, and you humanize both your project and your newfound relationship.

Who was the main character (or your leads) based on?

Why did you choose to write THIS story?

Why are you the only writer who could have written this very unique story?

What lives at the heart of the tale that will move us as audience (and that moved you to go to great lengths to write this screenplay)?

What will actors find so alluring about your characters?

Dig beneath the surface.

Get raw and honest, and tell the 'story behind the story' of your project.

When I submitted *The Mothman Prophecies* to Lakeshore Entertainment, I was aware the writer's agent had previously exposed that project to virtually every studio and independent film company in all of Hollywood. Everyone had passed on the project, which meant there was one and only one potential buyer left for this story.

The executive I'd spoken with and forwarded the script to was exceptionally bright, someone I respected a great deal. A few days later, she phoned to let me know she'd read the script, as had a couple of other executives at the company. While she found the story intriguing, it was going to be a pass for Lakeshore.

Knowing I had no other options, I requested a face-to-face meeting before they formally passed on this film. Less than a week later, I sat in a room with three members of the Lakeshore team to plead my case. I could not pitch the story, since they'd just read the script. Nor did it feel compelling to describe how we might improve the script.

The only thing that made sense, the only justification for taking these peoples' valuable time, was to share why I was so deeply attracted and connected to this material. Why was it so important for me personally to see this film produced?

I described a deeply personal experience, my relationship and friendship with my father, and how his passing forever changed my life. I shared my grief, the unexpected and surprising experiences that defined the next couple of years of my life, the shift that was at times marked by seemingly paranormal experiences and by heart-wrenching despair that felt like a crack in the universe, a deafening emptiness that forced me to explore a life I'd yet to imagine.

My experience was in no way unique. We all understand the devastating loss of those we love is every bit as much a part of our life journey as joy and love and celebration. I ended with a simple observation: everyone living today – including actors and filmmakers and audiences – will be moved by the story of *The Mothman Prophecies* because of our deeper humanity and the poignant reality of life and loss.

It involved only ten minutes or so of just talking, not really a traditional pitch, but it transformed that moment and story into something so raw, personal, moving and embracing of all people, that these executives changed their mind. They persuaded the head of Lakeshore and *The*

Mothman Prophecies was optioned, developed, purchased and produced with a stunning cast and director. To this day, I'm grateful to Lakeshore for taking a risk on a picture that was my private homage to my dad.

Though I've experienced amazing results from writers willing to share their personal *why*, this was the moment that forever cemented my belief that it's an imperative. Sharing yourself and your passions as an artist and as a person is a game changer. It draws people to you, whether that particular project goes forward or not. It humanizes you and makes you attractive in a more profound sense. Not sharing your 'why', your backstory (versus that of your lead character), only cheats you and whomever you're sitting with of a greater experience and relationship.

BEFORE YOU KNOCK …

Before you enter a meeting or make a phone call, of course, you'll want to do your homework. Research the person or people you're meeting with, their backgrounds and previous jobs, the company's team and projects or clients, their hometown and schools and achievements. If it's a producer who used to be an agent, that could be a wonderful pearl in your conversation… or where they're from, where they went to school. The more you know going in, the more naturally confident you'll feel. Google is your friend. *The Hollywood Reporter* and *Deadline* (both have online versions) are searchable and great ways to find press releases or any mention in an article of the person you're about to meet.

Research is alchemy. You'll inevitably feel more comfortable, very likely find common ground, and be able to ask appropriate questions that show you've cared enough to go out of your way to learn about them.

Creating the right mood or rhythm is fun - part improv, part being a great listener and being able to work off the energy of others, and part just putting yourself out there in a very authentic way. Consider it a date with someone you already know in advance really wants to go out with you – the opposite of a job interview. These folks take these meetings for one reason and one reason only, they're hoping to discover a great talent. They want to like you.

You're members of the same fraternity and share a common passion for brilliant storytelling, filmmaking, television. Create chemistry and warm up the room from the moment you set foot in their space. It's what any good storyteller wants to do to create a more receptive audience.

YOUR MISSION, SHOULD YOU CHOOSE TO ACCEPT IT...

Every meeting is a chance to share a piece of your story, to invite others to reciprocate, and to engage people on a deeper level that some would consider uncomfortable, if not daring. How good does it feel to leave a room knowing you've delivered the best of yourself? Leave people with the feeling that you're warm, authentic, engaging, thoughtful and fun. They will remember you, and that immediately separates you from the competition.

Most are so obsessed with leaving a room with a specific, immediate, short-term result, they forget to have fun, be themselves, do those things they'd do in any other context to begin building a relationship.

But not you. Because you understand that real, sustainable success comes from taking the opposite approach. You focus on making yourself a valuable currency, a person who knows their value, a personality that exudes confidence, creativity, openness and a happy disposition. You connect with people in a way that leaves them wanting more, regardless of whether this particular project, or the story, or the script is a good match for them. You're looking at a bigger canvas, a longer-term, more enduring success. And that's about you and the relationships you develop. All of which happens far more naturally and rapidly when you raise your energy, when you're good in the room, when you're so comfortable, relaxed and prepared that you're simply authentic and undeniable.

Whether you're meeting with one or three people, get them engaged in the moment, help them segue out of the litany of thoughts and calls and previous meetings. Simply distract them by being entertaining, enthusiastic, curious. Ask questions. When you ask a question, it immediately forces their subconscious to focus on you in that moment. It's a simple, invisible but powerful conversational tool. It also demonstrates your curiosity about them, which is both flattering and suggests confidence on your part.

No matter how busy people may appear, they truly want to be amazed by you and your story and, of course, your talent. Hollywood thrives on the discovery of new talent, and matching great talent to the right project.

No one takes meetings because they have gaps in their schedule; everyone's job and passion and interest (self-interest and company interest) is to find the incredible talent that not only solves their immediate problem, but can be another amazing turning point in their career.

Be on a mission to have fun, and make friends. From the second you walk in an office, smile and genuinely greet everyone as if each is the most important person in the room, beginning with the assistant. Make eye contact with everyone, stand tall but relaxed, shake hands and ask their names. Make a mental point to remember their names so you can thank each and every individual personally when the time comes to leave the meeting. There's no sound more pleasing to the human ear than the sound of one's own name. Here's your opportunity to do a small thing that will make a big impression.

People have great radar and they'll find your presence refreshing from the get-go if they see how relaxed and present you are. Truly be in the moment, be observant, be a detective, be a great storyteller, let them see you're just pleased as hell to be there.

And mean it. Just be real, be you, be authentic. These are the moments you live for, the connections you've been wanting to make, the opportunity to share your passion and personality and, ultimately, your talent.

CUROSITY WINS THE DAY

> *The cure for boredom is curiosity. There is no cure for curiosity.*
>
> ~ Dorothy Parker, author and renowned conversationalist

Be naturally curious. If you like people and are fascinated by their stories, if you enjoy discovering things about people, you're way ahead of the game.

Curiosity is one of the cornerstones of a successful life, and one of the preeminent qualities that bonds you immediately to people you're meeting for the first time. It communicates volumes about your confidence, humanity and professionalism. And it gives you a chance to listen and learn a great deal right off the bat (beginning with the assistant, whether you're on the phone or entering an office).

The more others are talking, the more they're engaged, and the more they'll subconsciously like you. Show genuine interest in others, ask questions, really focus when they're speaking, and people will naturally be more drawn to you.

The ability to listen deeply opens doors and creates opportunity. It seems silly to say, but it's sheer magic. It's one of the things most people rarely experience, because people tend to be consumed with telling their story, busy with their internal conversation, so much so that it deprives us of the opportunity to really get to know the person sitting across from us. People are talking all the time, but often not truly listening. People will notice when you do.

WARMING UP THE ROOM

When settling into a conversation or meeting, casually thank people for their time and acknowledge whoever setup the meeting. Slip in your excitement about the project and mention it by name. Then immediately shift into conversational mode, not into business mode. That subtle courtesy assures they'll recall who you are, the project to be discussed, how the meeting was organized, and who you know in common. If they've had a rash of meetings or calls prior to you arriving, this is a classy, gentle reminder of the context for this gathering.

The goal for every meeting should be to develop great rapport, regardless of whether or how often you get hired. If you succeed at creating friendly relationships out of those initial meetings, you've won. Period.

Make it fun and smart and it's very likely you'll be a repeat visitor to that office. If the producer, literary department coordinator, agent, manager or director later changes jobs or companies, see that as a positive. Your opportunity only expands. You maintain rapport with their former company as well, but now have inroads to new companies as well. That's only one reason it's important to stay in touch and track people's career paths.

Don't be overly focused on your own agenda. Go in prepared, knowing the purpose of the meeting and the part you play in it, knowing your material so well that you're not nervous or anxious, but really able to focus on the people in the room.

You'll get hired 99% of the time first because of who you are and how much people like and enjoy you, and secondly because of your talent or what you bring to the table professionally. The person who is the most fun, inspires the most confidence, tells the best story, and listens the best wins almost every time.

SETTING THE STAGE FOR MORE...

As a manager of talent, I noticed early on that once a client had one successful face-to-face meeting, more meetings almost always followed.

In this case, 'successful' meant the client felt prepared, comfortable, and confident, ready to engage with genuine curiosity, interest, ideas borne of research enabling them to put their best foot forward.

So it makes sense to make it as enjoyable, entertaining and 'winning' a moment as possible – separate and apart from the business at hand. That's the simple, subversive art of a great Hollywood meeting. Be the person they want to have back. Be charming, be relaxed, be likeable, be positive.

You may or may not be a perfect fit for a particular project, but you *may* be the perfect fit for their next project. They meet a lot of writers and directors, yes. And they can't say 'yes' to everyone in the moment. But they can say 'yes' to you as a person. They can invite you back for more meetings.

The more they learn about you, feel they know and enjoy you, the more likely they'll think of you. I've seen that happen again and again. So be prepared to enjoy yourself and give good meeting, creating a winning atmosphere.

THE RICHES OF RELATIONSHIP

Let me go back again to *The Mothman Prophecies,* since it is a great example. Over the course of meetings and phone conversations, I'd come to enjoy good rapport with two of the three executives that I met with at Lakeshore Entertainment that I met with to pitch this film project. I'd yet to successfully option or sell a script to Lakeshore, but had invested time getting to know them.

In hindsight, I could have looked at my investment of time with Lakeshore and their executives, including previous submissions and meetings, as a series of small failures. Or I could recognize that a 'yes' wasn't likely until I'd invested myself in getting to know them, and letting them get to know me. And that investment paid off in a big way. In the meeting, I was able to convince them this was a film that deserved to get made. I shared my passion for the project.

In that meeting, they changed their minds and committed to a budget of many millions of dollars. A year later, I produced a film that was personally very important to me. All because I'd made a priority of developing relationships. And for their trust and choices, I remain grateful to this day.

Remember, people want to be bowled over, blown away, swept away, amazed, speechless and excited. Everyone wants that! The opportunity and the magic begins the moment you walk through their door. Be committed to seizing opportunities and creating quality relationships on a regular basis.

LEAVE BEHIND

It's always a good idea to create a simple 'leave behind', a reminder document so the people you've just met with don't have to rely on their memory when relating your pitch to their boss, staff or team. This document will come in very handy at the conclusion of office pitch meetings or pitch fests. It's professional and, whether requested or not, a good tool to be able to offer to those you just pitched.

If emailing after a phone pitch or to the assistant at an office where you just had a meeting, paste your one-page 'leave behind' in the body of your email, rather than making it an attachment to your email. Make your communication as friendly as possible, requiring no extra steps or work on their part. If you are including additional material, e.g. the first ten pages of your screenplay, then it's fine to attach that to the bottom of your email.

Make certain your contact information appears prominently (a) at the bottom of your email, (b) at the top of your one-page 'leave behind', (c) on your screenplay's title page, and (d) on any other document or attachment. *Never* make someone search to find your phone or email or address. Your contact information may include: e-mail, e-fax or fax, address, phone, and URL for website if you have one dedicated to your writing. It's generally not a good idea to include URLs for your social media profiles, if any.

It seems common sense, but the number of queries, letters, emails, and messages sent via Facebook or other social media that fail to include this critical contact information is a perpetual source of frustration. For that reason alone, many will dispense with and not attempt response to your communication. No different than if you submit a letter or script with improper formatting, or with consistent misspellings, or a script that runs 130 pages. People quickly assess your professionalism from these not-so-subtle clues. So pay attention to form and substance, and certainly make it easy for people to say 'yes'.

And always opt for brevity. Re-read any communication – letter, 'leave behind' or synopsis - several times over a period of days. Find any word or phrase or sentence you can either delete because it's not essential, or you can improve. Ernest Hemingway once wrote a rambling 7-8 page letter to his editor, Maxwell E. Perkins. At letter's end, Hemingway signed off as follows: "Well, that's about it for now, Max. Please forgive me for writing such a long letter, but I didn't have the time to write a short one."

Please take the time to 'write a short one'. It will be noticed, appreciated, and more likely to receive response. This is one of the most common comments when talking with representatives or producers. They receive so much 'incoming' that a well-written, smart and concise communication is looked upon more favorably.

Similar to your query letter, begin your leave behind with your logline. Follow with your one-paragraph description or synopsis. If you feel it helps orient the reader, you can begin with 'a dramatic feature film screenplay' or whatever phrase is appropriate.

Include brief, pertinent information about your background. For example, it's better to focus on your writing background or that which makes you the perfect writer for this story, as opposed to extraneous, non-helpful facts such as degrees or other life credentials unless they directly relate to this specific project.

If you feel compelled to reference a screenplay competition or award, do not mention your numeric placement unless you were near the top (e.g. 'first' or 'second' place) or a 'finalist'. Similarly, do not reference dates unless the event took place quite recently.

Where appropriate, you can enclose a self-addressed, stamped envelope or postcard, which allows your reader a choice to respond by email, mail or phone, whichever is easiest for them.

BEFORE, DURING AND AFTER THE MEETING

The mechanics of a good meeting may seem self-evident, but worth going over briefly.

BEFORE

- Do your homework and research the people and company well ahead of time. If you find great tidbits (e.g. company history, current projects, where someone went to school), make conversational use of them. When they see you cared enough to learn about them, they'll feel flattered.
- Always arrive early (never **ever** be late for a meeting). Of course, you will print out and 'map' the address so there's no possibility of

getting lost. Plan on arriving at the office at least 5 or 10 minutes early, which will eliminate stress; given the unpredictability of traffic, that might mean arriving at the location 15 to 30 minutes ahead of time in order to get parked and up the elevator in a calm and collected state of mind. *(But under no circumstances enter an the office more than 10 minutes early.)* Arriving early also presents you a golden opportunity to learn what's going on in that office, learn names, observe personalities, and bond with the assistants.

- Get a business card or contact information for the assistant while you're waiting; ask questions or initiate conversation with the assistant or others while you're waiting, but always respectful not to interrupt if they're on the phone or busy. Be a detective and notice everything in their environment: artwork, awards, books, décor, anything with potentially useful information or conversational value.
- Turn off your cell phone.
- First impressions count, so show up as a professional, and present yourself in your best light. Be calm, confident, relaxed and smile.

DURING

- Make eye contact and greet and treat everyone the same, whether studio head or assistant. Introduce yourself by name, wearing that same smile, and remember (write down if you must) their names so you can thank them by name at meetings end as you're leaving.
- Be inclusive. Continue making eye contact with everyone, never focusing exclusively on whomever you think the most important person in the room. Be respectful and show you appreciate and value everyone's presence.
- When the meeting begins, thank them for meeting with you, and acknowledge anyone else who had a hand in organizing the meeting (e.g. your manager or agent).
- Have multiple copies of materials to share with those in the room. They may have received your materials in advance, but it's just good practice to always be prepared.
- Know the specific result (the desired outcome) you want from this meeting; for me, the big prize or most successful take-away is setting the stage for a follow-up conversation or meeting. Whatever it may be, your D.O. (discussed at length in Chapter 3) must be one item

only, not a shopping list. It must be simple, clear and achievable in that moment. Create your own reason to stay in touch, follow up, have a second meeting or next conversation. Keep the momentum alive by being creative and thoughtful.

- Know what outcome you want from a particular meeting but, as soon as you arrive, get *zen* and detach from your expectations so you're free to engage fully in the moment and genuinely enjoy the interaction without putting pressure on yourself.

- Wherever appropriate, ask a question that keeps people engaged and talking. Then let them have the floor. When you respond, make it about them or the company if you can, so you're not just re-focusing the conversation on you. Be smart, be strategic and be gracious.

- Don't overstay your welcome. If the meeting was scheduled for 20 minutes, take the initiative to thank them, let them know you appreciate their time, but it's been 20 minutes. If they want you to stay, they'll say so. Stay professional, confident, and in charge. Your conscious demeanor will stand out, be noticed and leave a strong positive impression.

AFTER

- Write and send a handwritten note or email thanking them again for their time. I encourage you to write separately to everyone you met, including the assistant, even if the assistant only greeted you and didn't actually join your meeting. Go the extra step and make the most of every opportunity to grow rapport and make a classy impression. Always include your full contact information. And make 100% certain to spell everyone's name correctly! It's a great reason to phone the assistant again and double-check the spelling of one or more names — and strike up yet another conversation.

- When emailing, as discussed in the chapter on Branding, I recommend a standard e-signature at the bottom of your message that includes your name, phone(s), and email address. If appropriate, include the URL for your website. Do not include links to your social media pages.

- Use the 'subject line' in an email to state your name, the project name, or some other reference that immediately tells the recipient who the email is from and what it's about. I get countless emails with a subject line that simply says 'hi' or 'thanks' or some other word or phrase that's not at all helpful. Take the time to establish relevance, thoughtfulness and clarity. People are more likely to respond well, consciously and subconsciously, when they know exactly who the message is from and what it concerns. Finally, always, *always* proofread your emails or other forms of correspondence before sending. Sloppy communication is not acceptable.

- As soon as you're outside the building or in your car (or off the phone call), make notes about who you met, the company, what was discussed, follow-up steps if any, and any other important observations. These notes become part of your history. You'll want to be able to share them with your representatives. You'll refer back to them when it comes time to meet these people again, whether at the same office or at a new company.

We discussed adages back on the first page of the chapter on networking. Here's another old adage: *it's not personal, it's business.* The new version of that adage is: *it's not business, it's personal.*

Make sure you make it personal.

MILESTONES

- View every phone call, email and in-person meeting as one part marketing and two parts being the personality people will want to invite back and get to know better.
- Do your homework. Before every meeting or phone call, research the person or people you're meeting with, their background and previous jobs, the company's team and projects or clients, their hometown and schools and achievements. Discover great pearls for conversation and questions, to impress them with your interest and effort. Feel confident before picking up the phone or walking into the room.
- Be warm, authentic, engaging, thoughtful and fun. Be open, charming and vulnerable, ask questions and be a good listener, share yourself authentically, let people see your true personality. Give them no choice but to remember you in your best light.
- Be genuinely curious about people, ask thoughtful questions, listen deeply to their responses, stay fully present (and don't worry) about what you'll say next.

- Be in the business of growing rapport and relationship wherever you go. Actively meeting quality people and marketing yourself inevitably leads to future results. Make it your mission to 'leave 'em wanting more'.
- Be professional, punctual, relaxed and smile. Learn everyone's name and make eye contact, making notes after every call and meeting to document all you've learned. Bond with the assistants, get business cards if available, thank everyone at the beginning and at the end of every meeting, and don't overstay your welcome.
- Make certain you always have enough (extra) materials, so every assistant or others you didn't expect in the meeting don't feel neglected.
- Prepare your desired outcome and follow-up in advance, so it becomes a natural and effortless part of your conversation.
- Send thank you notes (handwritten or email) as often as it feels appropriate.

So the major steps are under your belt: networking, branding, your D.O. list, recognizing the power of assistants (and the assistance they can bring to your career), the importance of building your dream team and protecting your work. You know your most powerful story and how to pitch it. What's the next step? Doing a little road-testing, that's what.

SUCCESS STRATEGY NINE: TESTING, TESTING... 1, 2, 3

Listen, wait, and be patient. Every shaman knows you have to deal with the fire that's in your audience's eye.

~ Ken Kesey, writer

TESTING

How do you know if something is working? Feedback from others. Because none of us are the best judge of our own work.

Success in a realm as subjective as intellectual property and storytelling requires you to be open-minded and to learn to crave and insist on feedback at each stage of your work. Before you begin marketing your project in earnest, do yourself a favor and solicit candid feedback from a diverse, smart group of friends and mentors in the business. This is equally true for your scripts, loglines, query letters, synopses, treatments, pitches and leave-behinds. Every item in your marketing toolkit deserves to be the best it can be. The only way to insure it's as good as it can be is to rely on the feedback and counsel of carefully selected people you admire, trust and respect.

Feedback loops are essential to our success as we prepare our arsenal of marketing tools. As in any business, if your customer (e.g. producers, agents, directors, talent, financiers, etc.) has a problem, it's your problem.

If ten people read your script and all of them offer different feedback, ranging from praise to criticism, that's a very very good sign. You'll merely want to pick the 'best of' and trust your creative intuition about which bits of feedback you incorporate and which you discard. If, however, ten people read your script and a majority offer consistent feedback, pay very, very close attention. They're right.

Get your ego out of the game and figure it out. This is not an intellectual process. It's about effective storytelling and that's as much a gut reaction as anything. This is a critical juncture that may foretell your success or lack thereof, so please remove your emotions and listen deeply when people offer feedback. If you don't immediately understand their comments, ask questions, probe a bit and do your best to understand your 'audience'.

Having friends and family read and react to your work has some legitimate, albeit limited value. It's better to seek the counsel of fellow writers, script consultants, assistants to or development executives for quality producers or agents or others, or a mastermind or writers forum if you happen to belong to one. This is the fastest and most reliable way to learn if you're on track or if you have to go back and rewrite yet some more.

If you've posted a logline and synopsis in a forum or on a site visited by professionals, and your materials have rarely been viewed after a handful of weeks, it may indicate your logline needs more work. Similarly, if people are clicking through to read your synopsis, but none are contacting you to request your screenplay, it suggests your synopsis may need additional rewriting.

FILMS, SCREENPLAYS AND EVERYTHING IN BETWEEN

Every film involves intense testing at each stage of the process.

In **pre-production**, table reads are a 'must'. They reveal how the story flows, how natural the dialogue sounds coming out of the actors' mouths, where the story seems to slow down, where people laugh or are surprised, and discover other reactions you might or might not be expecting. Beyond the cast who participate in the table read, the producer(s), writer, director, casting director and others involved in the production must all be in attendance to learn as much as possible and share thoughts about how to improve the screenplay before beginning production. Inevitably, table reads generate lots of discussion and story notes that the writer may do well to incorporate into the screenplay.

During **physical production or photography**, the director and producers and others view *dailies*, usually in the evenings after that day's schedule has been completed and production has wrapped. This is to insure there are no gaps in the story, to check that performances, lighting, sound and production values are solid, and that there's no need to re-shoot any of the day's footage.

The same holds true in **post-production**. Before the picture is *locked*, there are usually a multiple of test screenings for recruited audiences to assess their reactions and where additional editing is needed. Immediately following each test screening, a focus group is usually conducted. A certain number of audience members will be asked to stay after the screening to both fill out feedback forms, and answer 'live' a host of questions prepared in advance. After the Q+A session, the moderator will often open up the discussion and invite any and all feedback, ideas, criticisms, comments, suggestions. Once again, all this information is deemed vital and often triggers more editing and changes. The audience knows best!

But testing doesn't end when filming is complete.

Even when your film is released and in theatres – or your TV series begins to air –your marketing and ad campaign are constantly being tested, monitored, tweaked and revised.

THE SHARPER THE TOOL, THE BETTER THE RESULTS

No different than the film itself, each item in your marketing toolkit is a 'product' that deserves the same care and treatment. Each must be tested before you 'go to market', before you send any of these materials out to agents, casting directors, producers, directors, talent, financiers or executives. Treat each of your marketing tools as if the success of your project depends on the excellence of each individual tool (logline, synopsis, query, pitch, leave-behind, table read, etc.).

Arm yourself, your representatives, your producer, every member of your expanding team with world class tools. Don't be satisfied with the first or second version of any of these mission-critical items. Make every marketing piece 'shine', and the only way to achieve that is to repeatedly test and revise and refine multiple versions based on extensive feedback from experienced people. This is yet another rich opportunity to elevate people into your inner circle, by asking them in essence to be your mentor. It won't consume a great deal of their time, but the value of their input is priceless.

This is as good a reason as any to join a writer forum or mastermind group well before you need to ask any in the group for their advice. And when you do, don't ask for a favor, rather ask for their counsel. Slight difference in wording, a world of difference in how you're perceived and how motivated people will feel to say 'yes' to you.

Make a list of least five to ten trusted peers that you can regularly rely on for intelligent, thoughtful feedback about your work – be it logline, synopsis, your script itself, or your short film. If you haven't created this group and habit, it would be a good idea to begin making a list and refining that list of folks who you can rely on to be smart and constructive, and who'll devote the necessary amount of time to review your materials and give candid feedback. Consider mentors, forum members, teachers, script consultants (or a younger reader who works for a respected script consultant or for an agency).

Whoever you include in your "go to" group, let them know the huge value you place on honest feedback and criticism, and express your appreciation for their willingness to invest their time to read and give thoughtful reaction to your script.

TABLE READINGS

The *table read* may be the most under-valued, opportunity-rich tool you've not yet considered. At the highest levels of the film and TV business, no project enters production without benefit of a table read.

Actors literally sit around a table, each with a script where their character's dialogue has been highlighted, with a narrator to read the descriptions and scene transitions. The script is read aloud from beginning to end. Sometimes the table read is recorded on audio, sometimes on video.

If you intend to record a table read, whether audio or video, you'll want to have all present sign a one-paragraph document that grants you permission to do so.

At a minimum, the project's director, producer, writer, and casting director are present. Often, others have been invited to sit in as audience and observe, listen and give feedback after the reading is completed.

Hearing your work read aloud by talented actors (often the ones you'd ideally like to cast for the actual production) brings your project to life. It quickly reveals the strengths and weaknesses of your characters, plot, dialogue, story logic—what's working and what's not.

Beyond what you observe, after the reading you've a golden opportunity to canvas your cast, as well as your invited audience, to learn the strengths and weaknesses of your project. It's also a fun, creative and non-threatening environment that can work to get actors and others even more enthusiastic and emotionally attached to the project. Everyone experiences a greater sense of 'authorship' and engagement with your material.

Many years ago, I organized a table read of *Red Sneakers*, an independent film that I wanted to produce. I attached Cher to make her directorial debut, brought on board Mindy Marin, one of Hollywood's top casting directors, and together we assembled an exciting cast of some of the most sought-after younger actors at that time. We made no offers, no money changed hands, which ironically helped attract A-list talent to join together in what became a 'cause celebre'. The script was very well received, and came across beautifully and poignantly in this private table read moment. We invited friends to sit in as audience as well.

Here are some of the questions we asked our cast and audience at the conclusion of the reading.

- What moments stood out for you?
- What did you not understand?
- Where did the story seem long or slow for you?
- Did anything confuse you?
- Were there moments that passed too quickly?
- What did you like the most?
- What did you like the least?
- Were any lines of dialogue hard to say or unnatural feeling?
- Did any dialogue strike you as not fitting the character?
- Did any dialogue feel too "on the nose"?
- Which characters, if any, seem either underdeveloped or inconsistent?

Their responses not only helped us learn how to work with the writer to polish the screenplay, but the conversation itself created a sense of 'glue' that bonded everyone in the room to one another and to the material.

For unrelated reasons, the project did not go forward, but that single experience burned into my professional psyche a determination to table read every single project I would develop from that day forward. The benefits were so immediate, on so many levels, human and creative and practical, that the table read became something far greater than a tool to learn how to improve a script. That was just the appetizer. I cannot imagine ever producing a short film, stage play, a film or TV comedy or drama without taking advantage of this amazing, fun, rich opportunity.

It doesn't matter if you're a writer, producer, director or hyphenate. Gift yourself the experience of organizing a table read that will deepen and expand your relationships, give you carte blanche to call creative talent and invite them to participate in an experience that is irresistible to most, and learn so much from this 'live' and out loud dramatization of your script. The same goes for invited audience. People in the business are not often invited to a live table read. This is your chance to reach out to other actors, editors, cinematographers, production designers, producers, virtually anyone you think might be a good creative or strategic 'fit' – either because they could become involved, or merely give extraordinarily insightful feedback, or possibly refer or recommend others that would be a perfect 'fit' for your project or for you (e.g. maybe their representative). It's the perfect way to create 'buzz' and let positive word of mouth travel quickly in unimagined directions.

When we did a table read at the Sundance Institute's Production Lab for *3000* (later renamed *Pretty Woman*), Paul Hirsch was in attendance. Paul's achievements as an editor are legendary, including *Star Wars*, Ray, *Mission Impossible*, *Ferris Bueller's Day Off*, *Steel Magnolias*, and *Mighty Joe Young*, among more than 40 films, many of which were huge commercial and critical successes. I've no idea how many awards Paul has won, deservedly so, but his creative input was beyond anything I'd experienced to date. Approaching people of that caliber as a mentor is a dream opportunity and the table read is an ideal environment that requires only a couple of hours of their time.

> *Each item in your marketing toolkit deserves the same*
> *exacting level of care you would apply to your scripts;*
> *and each must be tested, and not just once, before 'going*
> *to market'. Your success depends to a great extent on the*
> *excellence of your marketing materials.*
>
> ~ Gary W. Goldstein

MILESTONES

- None of us are the best or most objective judge of our own work, so it's critical to test every element in your marketing toolkit – scripts, loglines, query letters, synopses, treatments, pitches, and leave-behinds – with vigilance, on an ongoing basis.
- Carefully select and solicit feedback from people you admire, trust and respect, and who have the experience to offer quality counsel; five or more advisors is a reliable number and offers you a range of smart opinion.
- If your inner circle offers diverse, inconsistent feedback, choose the

'best of' and use your intuition about what you elect to incorporate or disregard; if, however, a majority of your peers, mentors, or other 'pros' offer consistent feedback, listen very carefully and take their comments to heart.

So you not only know your most powerful story, you know how to pitch it. You've tested it, as you have all your marketing tools. Now it's time to pick up a camera.

Hey, kids, let's put on a show!

SUCCESS STRATEGY TEN: CREATE YOUR OWN CONTENT AND TAKE CONTROL

It starts with the writer--it's a familiar dictum, but somehow it keeps getting forgotten along the way.

~ Steven Spielberg

It's a fact: if you create your own content, market it cleverly, you will get noticed in a way that writers who are merely waiting on others to take action simply won't be.

Talent's great. Effectively marketed talent is the stuff of a truly enduring career. And that's the big divide.

Writers (and every creative talent) should be creating, producing, marketing and distributing their own short content. Especially in today's digital world, where access and dollars and crews are no longer an obstacle. Every tool and strategy you can imagine is available to you at little or no cost.

You have everything you need today to grant yourself absolute permission to 'do it yourself'. Certainly it's up to you to create new relationships, to market yourself, to put your strategies into action daily. It's also up to you – if you intend to be one of the few who distinguish themselves – to take extraordinary action, assemble others to aid and abet your mission to create a short film, a web series, even a feature length film.

Getting yourself out there, branding and marketing yourself, and showcasing your talent should be your number one priority... and it's 100% do-able. Those who don't aren't stopped because they need a significant budget or expensive equipment or fancy post-production or talented crew. They stop themselves because they don't think they're capable. Because it seems like a lot of work. Because they don't recognize that it's their obligation to create content, to give themselves a leg up in the marketplace, to market themselves in the first place.

NO BARRIER TO ENTRY

It requires very little money. There are hundreds of talented directors, editors, actors and crew near you who'd jump at the chance to collaborate with you to create a short film. Beyond a handful or two of collaborators, a simple camera and editing software are all you'll need. And it's fun.

The first film I ever produced cost $200,000 because we had a large cast and crew, shot on traditional Panavision film cameras in over 30 locations, edited the old fashioned (non-digital, expensive) way. You get the picture. Streamline the story, the size of the cast, use the digital cameras and editing technology that's available and so cheap today, and it might cost a fraction of that amount. And that's for a full-length feature film.

Technology and equipment, web marketing, ways to quickly discover and align with quality collaborators – all these things are at your fingertips and virtually cost-free. All you have to do is be willing, be determined, create a plan, and take action. Everything you need is a keystroke away.

If you don't know how to operate a camera, no problem. If you don't have a cast, a director, or a cinematographer, no problem. Post your project needs in an online forum or on Craigslist or at a local film school and watch what happens. Today, you can attract who and what you need – efficiently, smartly, and quickly.

Beyond your own finished short film itself, you'll reap the rewards of new relationships and you'll learn from your new-found collaborators and friends. Your marketing toolkit and your confidence level will automatically upgrade from coach to first class.

D.I.Y.

'DIY' – do it yourself – is a movement, a fast-growing reality, the way so much is being created and put out on the web, on television, and in theatres. There are plentiful examples in every category of entertainment. Here are just a few:

Sanctuary

This science fiction series, the earliest webisodes of which were stunningly well produced, initially aired on the web. After a handful of segments, this web-series got picked up by the Sci-Fi Channel (now Syfy) and was no longer a web wannabe. While a webby show, it amassed a huge following, the very reason it got picked up, and it ran for four season on Syfy. Is it possible? Absolutely. Is it happening with greater frequency? Yes.

Signs

A 12 minute short with no dialogue, this remarkable little film won a gold medal at the 2009 Cannes Lions Festival. You can watch it on YouTube. As good a film as it is, and it's inspired for its elegant simplicity and visual storytelling, you may say to yourself 'I could have made that film'. And yes, you could and can and should.

Once

This amazing 2006 feature film out of Dublin was made for U.S. $160,000 with only two handheld cameras. Starring Glen Hansard of the Irish rock band The Frames (hardly a household name), the film won the Independent Spirit Award as Best Foreign Film, an Oscar for Best Original Song, and was picked up for U.S. distribution by Fox Searchlight. Neither the male nor female lead was a trained actor, and the film's director (the former bassist for the same rock band, The Frames) was a first-timer. The film was shot with a skeleton crew on a 17 day shoot, using all natural light and friends' homes as locations. Turned down by multiple European film festivals, it was picked up for a screening at Sundance and the rest, as they say, is history.

As of 2010, the film had achieved $9.5 million at the U.S. box office and almost $21 million at the worldwide box office. All on a budget of $160,000. It was "the little film that could".

Having seen the film, Steven Spielberg was quoted as saying "A little movie called *Once* gave me enough inspiration to last the rest of the year". All this for a film that couldn't get arrested, whose original financing (over 3 times the amount of money it was eventually produced for) fell through. The film garnered consistent rave reviews from critics and audiences, despite a team of would-be filmmakers with no track record, no big budget, no distribution, but a whole lot of inspiration, persistence, belief and guts.

But the accolades didn't stop there: in the summer of 2011, *Once* went into development in the New York Theatre Workshop, and opened late that year Off-Broadway. It then transferred to Broadway in the spring of

2012, opening to rave reviews, and led the season's list of musicals with nominations for eleven Tony awards. *Once* brought home eight of those awards – including Best Musical – and seems destined not only for a long Broadway run (and national tour), but for a substantial – and, for its creators, consistently income generating – 'afterlife' in community and university theatres across the country.

Paranormal Activity

On his first film, Oren Peli served as the film's writer, director, producer, cinematographer, editor and casting director. Oren went 50% over his original budget of $10,000, and ended up spending $15,000 by the time all was said and done. The 2007 film skyrocketed to over $107 Million at the U.S. box office, plus another $85 Million internationally, bringing in almost $200 Million, not including DVD or other revenue streams. (Listen to the filmmaker's commentary on DVD to learn the amazing story of how his film came to be released by Paramount.) Be sure to take a look at his listing on IMDb to get further details on his three sequels to *Paranormal Activity*, his *three* other feature films either in production or in release, and the *eight* episodes of the network television series he wrote and produced. All these results are the return on Oren Peli's involvement, on his willingness to take action and "do it himself". That's his and your potential return on an investment of $15,000 !

Four-Eyed Monsters

Initially leaked over the web as episodes, this 2005 film became famous when the producers used video podcasts to get the word out, then released the film for free on YouTube and MySpace. It received over a million views. The producers then offered audiences the opportunity to attend a screening in their hometown if they'd just go online and request a screening. That email list was the powerful social proof that allowed the film to secure a distribution deal with IFC, and a theatrical run in the U.S.

IT'S YOURS FOR THE DOING

Can you be the architect of your own success? Absolutely!

The above examples are just a very few of the many instances where artists took matters into their own hands. No permission, just belief, sweat, massive action, enlisting whoever they needed along the way to realize their dream.

DIY success stories are happening in ever greater numbers. It's the new game of TV and film for writers, directors, producers, actors – for every kind of storyteller. As viewing habits migrate across devices and online, it's no longer essential to have traditional distribution in place to achieve outsized success.

These creatives – the ones who conceived and created *Sanctuary*, *Signs, Once,* and countless other indie projects – did not view marketing themselves and their projects as a lesser pursuit or as activities reserved for agents or others to perform on their behalf. These are the five percent who are excited and not content to wait or put off an opportunity until tomorrow.

Your skill as a writer deserves to be supported by your commitment to becoming that kind of skilled marketer. Surround yourself with mentors, and a variety of successful folks with positive attitudes. Be discerning as you expand your network. Cast a smarter, wider net. Seek the counsel and friendship of people you want to be around. Use your precious time strategically and intentionally.

Beyond that, ask: 'How can I take matters into my own hands?'. Can you shoot a short? Yes. If you don't have a handheld semi-professional camera, buy a video camera, borrow a camera from a friend, do whatever it takes. It doesn't matter how you capture your story, so long as you have a go at it. If that sounds like you, if that excites you, make a decision. You either know or can find people who can help you. Maybe you don't want to direct it yourself or wear other hats, but you can find and attract a team of motivated, dedicated, talented folks who will pitch in to get your project made. Start today. Even if you've yet to complete a finished script, set the intention to create your short content and begin reaching out to potential collaborators. Start the conversation and magnetize good people to support you.

Creative people are looking for every opportunity to exercise their craft. They're not looking for reasons to stay home. So step it up, get excited about your vision and be a fierce and disciplined marketer and storyteller. Ask people for help, and let them see your determination and passion. Be persistence personified and take charge.

THE OPPORTUNITY

Unlike even a handful of years ago, we no longer have to run up huge credit card bills to finance professional quality HD video productions.

Today it can be 'cost neutral' (free). A used video camera might cost $100, or you can borrow someone's camera, and essentially instantly have your own movie studio. Unlike in the past, it's not complicated to shoot and produce video. There's no longer anything or anybody standing in your way, other than… you.

But it gets better. Today, we can create our own content - short films, webisodes or otherwise - and not stop there. Through the Internet, we have free access to countless social media and other platforms to host our content, distribute our content, and quickly attract a growing audience and fan base.

And that's a powerful career strategy, especially in tandem with the other strategies in this book that empower you to consistently be creating relationships and gaining access to the professional communities within Hollywood.

Many are producing videos for free and monetizing them on YouTube, their own websites or elsewhere. You can too.

My friend, Bob Fraser, described a young woman in Australia who'd been shooting short videos with just a Flip video camera. In 2010, she earned revenues in excess of $200,000 (her share of advertising revenue, based on the number of fans who regularly went online to see her short films).

Whether your plan includes generating revenue from your webisodes or other short content, you win big by creating a visual and compelling marketing tool few others will be bold enough to undertake. Captivating short content that bears your creative signature is a stand-out way to meet more Hollywood pros on your Top 100 list, and grow an audience or fan base at the same time.

It's worth taking the time to listen to the speech by **Joss Whedon** – best known as the creator of the phenomenally successful TV series *Buffy the Vampire Slayer* – when he accepted the 2009 Streamy Awards for Best Directing in a Comedy Web Series for his tremendously successful *Dr. Horrible's Sing-Along Blog* (which he co-wrote as well). He confirms that people independently creating content for the Internet are, in fact, creating our future media landscape. This is where we're headed, and we don't need huge budgets to shoot our series and our short films and our feature length films today.

Now that's what I call opportunity!

THINK BIG, THEN THINK AND PLAN BIGGER

Whenever you set out to do what most aren't willing to do, it's because you have a plan for an uncommon success. The vast majority may dream, but you plan and follow through with persistent, smart actions.

So what's really possible? What results can you realistically plan in advance and build into your goals and business plan for your short film?

Let's set the bar high:

a. you will attract better meetings based on the quality of your short film;

b. you'll attract a quality team, including the caliber of agent that can truly make a difference for your career;

c. you'll forge important working relationships with other talents, including directors and cinematographers, as a result of collaborating on your short film;

Now set the bar higher:

d. your film will be accepted and be screened in competition at the Sundance Film Festival or win at the Cannes Film Festival; and

e. your film will make the 'short list' for next year's Oscars. Someone's film does. Why not yours?

At the end of the game, it's the director who will attract the actors and it's the script that will attract the director. It all starts with the screenplay.

~ David Brown, producer

THE ELEMENTS FOR YOUR SUCCESS

Concept Can't cheat here. You cannot get to the promised land by taking shortcuts. The concept and DNA of your film <u>must</u> embrace exceptional, brilliant, amazing, breathtakingly interesting characters. Comedy or drama, the same holds true. Authenticity is key, dialogue is spare. The concept must be wholly fresh and feel new, unique, special, exceptional. Does it truly excel at what it purports to be? Whether original comedy that's simply funny and surprising, a character piece that takes audiences on an unexpected and powerful journey, or a socially conscious story that 'gets us where we live', the concept and characters should be the stuff of audience-pleasing brilliance.

Story and Script Again, nothing shy of brilliance. When the idea first strikes you, you feel exhilarated, as if you're experiencing magic itself. By the time you've crafted it, there's nothing ordinary about the characters, story, dialogue, tapestry and arc of the journey. It's pure inspiration and can translate into a film that will surprise, delight and amaze. You intuitively know how to tell this story in the visual medium of film (aka HD video) in 7-12 minutes, possibly even a shorter running time. Given that length, the story needs be told without preamble, without overwrought setup or introduction. It takes us immediately into the heart and action of the journey. Think film haiku.

Impeccable Elements Reach for the moon. If you fall short, you'll still be among the stars. Your choice of actors, director, cinematographer, editor, location(s) and music should exceed what people typically expect from a short film. If your concept and story defy expectation, are truly original, authentic and excellent, you have the upper hand and advantage. Top talent responds to extraordinary storytelling. You can entice them with your story, all the while only needing their services for a day or several days at most.

Knowing this, aim as high as you can. Dream big and dare to approach people most wouldn't even consider. Some will say 'no', certainly. But persist because some will say 'yes'. Make a list of your top 10 choices for every category mentioned above. Use every skill you've learned in this book to find your way to them. Don't underestimate the elements that make for an outstanding film experience: your choice of music and composer, a gifted editor, first-rate lighting and sound.

Marketing and Dollars Have a plan. Most filmmakers and talent who make any film, feature length or short, fall down when it comes to having a smart action plan to market their film when it's ready to be unveiled. Much can be done for free, but have a modest marketing budget to support you in creating:

- a professional quality press release;
- simple but compelling online/offline collateral material;
- a compelling trailer for your film (for use on your website and on YouTube, etc.);
- a simple web presence (website and social media presence on Twitter, Facebook, etc.);

- optional would be a reasonable number of professionally duplicated DVDs (to submit to key influencers, film festivals, reviewers, executives, etc.);
- film festival submission fees;
- a publicist or someone to help create online buzz using social media, and submit to reviewers, major film blogs, as well as traditional media and journalists; and
- to cover any other critical items you've planned in advance and included in your budget.

Outreach Early on, begin researching and identifying two items. First, the person or team who excels at marketing, publicity and grassroots promotion (i.e. not expensive, retainer-based traditional Hollywood PR firms). Second, research the best film festivals in the world, which boast short categories (most of the high end festivals certainly do), and prioritize which you want to target and in which order. Prepare to submit to at least a few handfuls of the best of the best. Don't wait. Begin to open doors and find your way into conversations and rapport with the short film programmers or others associated with your 'target' festivals early on. Relationships help successfully navigate those opportunities, assuming your finished film is world-class entertainment.

And remember, simplicity is a virtue, especially when it comes to storytelling.

> *Perfection is achieved, not when there is nothing more to add, but when there is nothing left to take away.*

~ Antoine de Saint-Exupery

MILESTONES

- Nothing says 'you' better than your words and talent transferred into an entertaining short. It also communicates volumes about you – you're a 'doer', someone who's committed and willing to do whatever it takes to 'make it' in the film and TV business.
- Finding motivated and talented collaborators, as well as equipment, wherever you are can be done virtually, quickly and with no expense. For short content shot on a shoestring budget and

accelerated schedule, you'll likely discover talent who are willing to forego compensation to gain experience and to expand their 'reel' or portfolio.

- Short content is your shortcut to better meetings, to introduce yourself to more quality people (you can email a link to your content or send a DVD), and to enter film festivals where you can meet even more 'insiders' and get noticed.

So we've covered the strategies you'll need, and you've learned a few techniques along the way. You not only know your most powerful story, you can pitch it with the best of them. Now that you've made your own short film, you've got the goods to show off your talent. What could possibly be next?

Earning your own PHD – in Pig Headed Determination.

SUCCESS STRATEGY ELEVEN: PERSISTENCE... a/k/a PIG-HEADED DETERMINATION

Gain The Slight Edge That Multiplies Results Over Time

Results? Why, man, I have gotten lots of results!

If I find 10,000 ways something won't work, I haven't failed.

I am not discouraged, because every wrong attempt discarded is often a step forward....

~ Thomas Edison, inventor

Thomas Edison's statement has an unavoidable requirement attached to it: Pig-headed determination. Consistent persistence. Never quitting.

FABULOUS FAILURES PAVE THE WAY TO SUCCESS

Here are some remarkable facts about early obstacles and the magnificent failures faced by creatives who've gone on to succeed at the highest levels and made great and lasting contributions:

J.K. Rowling's initial *Harry Potter* manuscript was rejected by twelve publishers before a tiny London publisher picked it up for publication.

Walt Disney was fired by a newspaper editor who said "he lacked imagination and had no good ideas". Disney would later say "all our dreams can come true, if only we have the courage to pursue them".

The Beatles were rejected by Decca Records who said "we don't like their sound".

Elvis Presley was kicked out of the Grand Ole Opry with a recommendation he go back to driving a truck.

It took **Jane Austen** 17 years to find a publisher for 'Pride and Prejudice'.

Zen and the Art of Motorcycle Maintenance, **Robert Pirsig's** renowned best seller, was rejected by 121 publishers before being accepted by Viking Press.

Julia Roberts auditioned for *All My Children* – but didn't get the part.

Brad Pitt's first acting job was wearing a chicken suit to attract customers to El Pollo Loco restaurant.

What kept them going? What will keep *you* going?

For me, it's having a smart plan and knowing exactly, specifically and precisely what are the 3 to 5 things I will do tomorrow, come rain or shine, that will lay the foundation for my next success.

It's that simple. It's in the doing, not in the thinking about doing. My belief in this is absolute, because it's worked for me and every successful person I know.

I choose to ignore the toe-stubbing and the naysayers. I choose to not feel defeated by but rather to learn from my failures. I choose to believe in me.

As Thomas J. Watson Sr., founder of IBM said:

> *Would you like me to give you a formula for success? It's quite simple, really. Double your rate of failure. You are thinking of failure as the enemy of success. But it isn't at all. You can be discouraged by failure or you can learn from it.*
>
> *So go ahead and make mistakes. Make all you can.*
> *Because remember that's where you will find success.*

THE NEW BABYLON

As my first foray into the film business after moving to Los Angeles, I optioned the rights to *The New Babylon*, a beautifully photographed silent film from 1929 which tells a sweeping story set in the Paris Commune of the 1870s. I planned to open the film in the grandest renovated theatre in Columbus, Ohio, where the film's brilliant Shostakovich score would be performed live by the Columbus Symphony. I hired the teamsters. I produced radio and TV spots. I ran newspaper ads and put up posters.

This would be my grand entrance into the entertainment world. It would make headlines as a cultural high-water mark, the most exciting film event to tour the U.S. since Coppola's 'Napoleon'.

The result: I lost $80,000 in the first weekend.

Most of that money was borrowed. Back then, that amount felt like millions, not thousands of dollars.

I couldn't imagine how I'd dig out from that disaster. I flew back to Los Angeles, tail between legs, and decided the only direction to move was forward. Over the next several years, I struggled to paid my debts and, slowly, like a stubborn little snail, built a successful business. Brick by brick. At the time, I knew nothing about the business of Hollywood, and knew zero people in film or TV.

The big lesson I learned in Columbus, Ohio, was how desperately I needed mentors in my life. I needed to develop relationships with as many smart, successful people as I could find. Whatever it took. I wasn't about to quit.

A BLACK BELT AT FAILURE

My failures or obstacles have been a constant for as many years as I can remember. I've become a black belt at failure, and that's paved the way for my successes.

It's up to you how you classify or view any moment or event. Every film I've ever championed was a failure many times before I ultimately got it produced. For every film I've produced, there are another six or ten films I failed to get produced; I invested years of my time, plenty of money, and a big piece of me in those as well. There are films I worked on for years and years before it became absolutely impossible, legally or financially or practically, to get that particular film into production. Until that moment arrived, I never quit. Never.

Over the years, I learned to fall in love with my failures. I feel proud to have earned my black belt in failure. That's where I learned, that's where I tested my own character and resolve, grew countless enduring relationships, and basically turned the earth to grow more success.

Were the films I developed but failed to get produced any less compelling than the ones I did get produced? Not in my view. And even the successful films had a history of falling apart repeatedly.

Pretty Woman stalled at two separate companies before I was able to

> ## ADVICE FROM A MASTER
>
> Isaac Asimov, the prolific science fiction and science writer who published or edited over 500 books, including the famed *I, Robot*, once said:
>
> "You must keep sending work out; you must never let a manuscript do nothing but eat its head off in a drawer. You send that work out again and again, while you're working on another one. If you have talent, you will receive some measure of success - but only if you persist."

set it up at Touchstone (Disney). One of those companies declared bankruptcy and the project came close to being buried for years, if not forever. Richard Gere had turned the project down. Disney wasn't initially keen on Julia Roberts. For three years, the film flirted with failure. The circumstances that allowed the film to come together at Touchstone with Garry Marshall, a dream director, and with Julia Roberts and Richard Gere, the very cast I'd dreamt about since I first held the script in my hand, were nothing short of miraculous.

The Mothman Prophecies had been passed on by every major studio and independent film company in all of Hollywood, with one exception. By the time the script came to me, there was one and only one potential production company that could say 'yes' and finance the project. And then that company passed on the script. Relationship and persistence are the currencies that allowed me to push past the 'pass', ask for a face-to-face meeting and turn that project's fate around.

Every film's history, every screenwriter's backstory, every actor's career, is pockmarked with a long string of rejections and temporary defeats. It's just a reality I've come to expect and take as neither good nor bad. I accept and embrace it, and choose to stay focused and flexible and very pig-headed.

I place a far greater value on persistence and my belief in a writer or in a project than any wave of rejections. The wave will pass, but my belief remains intact. Some who rejected my project this time around will either be talking about it to others or likely open to championing my next project. Success in life is not a lottery, it's a campaign. Life is a process, not an event.

When asked in an interview to describe the experience of making a film, Norman Mailer replied: "Making a film is a cross between a circus, a military campaign, a nightmare, an orgy and a high". The greater truth is the analogy to a military campaign. Having a plan, executing that plan, day in and day out, is what will win the day.

YOUR PERSONAL CAMPAIGN

My responsibility is to stay on mission, believe in myself, take consistent persistent smart action, and continue my campaign until successful. Each 'no' brings me closer to my 'yes'. Imperfect action wins over perfect inaction. The worst case is I continually develop more good relationships that make the next project more viable, more likely to meet with a positive outcome.

Jeffrey Katzenberg, former Chairman of Walt Disney Studios, famously said "If they throw you out the door, climb in a window. If they throw you out the window, get in through the basement, but find a way in!". And that sums up what it takes to make it in Hollywood and elsewhere. You just want it more, and are willing to fail more and get up more often than most human beings.

DON'T WAIT FOR PERMISSION, DON'T WAIT TO BE DISCOVERED

And that's the crux of it. If you're expecting your talent to be discovered in your first meeting or pitch, then you're setting yourself up for disappointment. If you're willing to dig in for the long haul, do the hard work, make relationships, constantly improve at your craft, shrug off the 'passes' and 'no's' and keep moving forward every day with your plan, the game is yours to win.

The winner in life has a simple formula: just keep getting up. The winner's simple edge is being willing to get up one more time than those around them, all those who defeat themselves too soon.

The road to *yes* is littered with roadblocks labeled *no*. You simply can't get there without taking the whole journey. Along the way, the key is to meet people, keep going, treat every apparent disappointment as an opportunity to learn, show your character, and enhance every relationship.

THE 'F' WORD

Failure and success are simply yin and yang; siblings separated at birth, and failure is just the one who got a bad rap. Success and failure cannot be divided— nor should they be. They live on a continuum of our experience, throughout our lives. Failure is every bit if not more crucial to our growth and our lifelong learning. My failures have shaped me far more than my successes. They've been the better teacher and made me believe more in myself.

The only thing that divides me, you or anyone from everyone else who lives with regret is that we put our shoulder behind our dreams, we try, we fall down and get back up, we try again, we fail until we succeed.

Success is built one brick at a time. Success is just that mundane. Inwardly, it's a fierce, exciting, exhilarating exercise, every day waking with a sense of purpose that you translate with excitement into actual deeds, tasks, conversations. Putting one foot in front of the other, you see clearly where you're going and that's all you need to stay inspired and in motion.

The majority of folks expect and anticipate defeat. They don't believe in themselves enough. They're too busy listening to that Greek chorus of voices in their head that chant about self-doubt, about all the reasons 'why not'. They're the majority who've joined with the naysayers around them, the 95% who walk through their lives not achieving their potential, the ones who later suffer the crushing pain of regret.

The majority choose reasons over results. They're more comfortable justifying their failures than being pig-headed enough to fight through to their successes.

The simple secret is to just get up, dust yourself off, and go at it again. After all, what's a nick or a bruise? When you learned to ride a bicycle for the first time, a scraped knee never stopped you, never overshadowed your excitement and determination to ride that bicycle.

Never allow yourself more than a moment to reflect on the negative feelings around a failure. Rather, congratulate yourself for being in the game, for having a go at it, and prepare to go again. With whatever you just learned, immediately charge back into the fray.

As best-selling author and marketing guru Seth Godin says: "Persistence isn't using the same tactics over and over again. That's just annoying. Persistence is having the same *goal* over and over."

WHO'S IN YOUR HEAD AND SUPPORT CIRCLE?

Persistence is motored by belief. While belief starts within yourself, your social support network will go a long way to reinforcing your belief and ability to persist. It's okay to let those who don't support you gently fade from your inner circle.

Mark Twain cautioned "Keep away from people who try to belittle your ambitions. Small people always do that, but the really great make you feel that you too can become great." Surround yourself with those who see you for who you can be, and you'll become the person you were destined to be.

THE DECENT PLAN YOU EXECUTE vs. THE PERFECT PLAN YOU QUIT

Look in the mirror and see your bigger self, your true self, the person you know in your gut and heart that you were meant to be. Make a vow that this day and every day from here on in, you will take one or more actions to transform your plans into concrete reality. It's not important whether each effort yields short-term success. Ted Williams, one of the greatest batters in the history of baseball, failed 6 out of every 10 times at bat. Persistence was all that made him a superstar, and got him into the Hall of Fame.

Take daily action, small simple but conscious and measurable steps to bring you closer to your goals. Set big goals for yourself, *big audacious goals*, goals others might scoff at or think beyond reach. If you set goals that are too easy to achieve, they don't serve you at all. Set big goals, audacious goals, force yourself into simple habits that grow you into the biggest version of yourself.

Taking action day by day, week by week, month by month grows your confidence, belief and results. This is your mission, mandate, obligation and responsibility to yourself. This is the joy of this precious time we have, to become and rejoice in becoming the person you know is dying to be expressed, to make a bigger contribution, be self-determining, not waiting on permission, not acquiescing to those little voices of doubt and insecurity that would have you live safely in a closet the rest of your life. It's up to each of us to transform our dreams into reality.

I look at each of you and see only possibility. Most suffer 'possibility blindness' because they believe a lesser story about themselves and their capacity for a bigger, ever more successful life. But those limiting beliefs are just that, a made up story. Change your self-story and limits evaporate. Create a new story of who you are, who you're entitled to be in the world. If it were easy, the successful would vastly outnumber the unsuccessful and unfulfilled. At most, one out of twenty embrace their bigger possibility, believe in themselves, exercise the habit of discipline, take daily action and stay the course. Commit to being extraordinary, to live among the top 5% who thrive and succeed because they simply won't quit.

It's worth repeating the wisdom of Dag Hammarskjöld, diplomat and author:

> *Never measure the height of a mountain until you have reached the top.*
>
> *Then you will see how low it was.*

What seems so daunting initially, is not at all intimidating in hindsight. Our character and capacity and confidence expand to whatever dimensions we desire. Give yourself a huge challenge, a massive set of goals, an environment others would shrink from, and grow yourself to suit your mission. Live a quiet, safe life with modest goals, and you won't need to grow very much because you won't require it of yourself.

MAKE A CHOICE TO LEAVE THE 95% AND JOIN THE 5%

Every day you choose not to perform the tasks that help move you forward is a day you avoid success. This is about the geometry of time and success. 5% will commit and 95% will find a reason not to commit. Choose to be uncomfortable, to stretch yourself, to do those things that it might be easier to procrastinate or avoid altogether. You're definitely in control.

In the quiet of evening, make a list of the people you'll contact the next day, the mentors you'll seek out, the companies you'll target, the events you could attend, the book you'll read, the emails and letters you'll send, the phone calls you'll make.

Some refer to this as your '10 by 10'. Successful people literally plot out the most important things they need to accomplish by a certain hour the next day to move closer to their goal. It might not be 10 things, it might not be by 10 am. You design the system that works for you.

The key is to not let distractions take over your day. Don't let lack of focus hijack you from your mission. Allow emails to go unanswered, phone calls unreturned, Facebook ignored until you've done whatever you decide is critical to make this day a success for you. Because what you think and what you do, multiplied by time, will determine what you get.

Align your values, your goals and your actions so you take a step in a positive direction every day, no matter how small. Even a failed step is a positive step. Inaction is the only failure. Taking yourself out of the game is the only certain way to fail.

Decide what you want, when you want it, how you'll get there, choose a team, choose strategies. Chunk it down so your goals are broken into tiny bite-size pieces, clear actions that will individually and collectively give you the results you want.

A while back, I received an email that read as follows: "While searching for people to read my work, I concluded that to break into Hollywood it takes: 60% luck, 39% persistence, and 1% talent".

The person who wrote me that email had the right idea. Unfortunately, he had the numbers backwards. Imagine what a different attitude, what different results, how different the people he would attract into his life, if instead he'd written and believed that to succeed, whether to break into Hollywood or otherwise, it takes: 60% persistence, 39% talent, and 1% luck.

CHOOSE WISELY

In life, everyone gets to choose. You can have reasons or you can have results. Each of us creates our own lucky breaks and that's what makes this experience called life so exciting. Luck is something we create by design, with preparation and hard work.

Social psychology has proven that attitude is far more predictive of success than intelligence or talent. Persistence results from a positive attitude, from being optimistic and seeing opportunity, people and circumstances through a positive lens. As experts are now positing, it may well be that talent or skills represent at most 25% of our potential for long-term success.

If we prepare, if we step onto and stay on the path of our own mastery, opportunity is the natural consequence. Market yourself well, intentionally grow the greatest possible number of quality relationships and friendships with successful people, and greater success becomes predictable. Stay home, literally and figuratively, waiting for the phone to ring, and you'll be met by silence. The math of the universe is simple, straightforward, predictable and eternal.

We live in an age where everyone seems to expect overnight, instant success and results. But true success is earned, not indiscriminately handed out to the 'lucky' as if life were a lottery.

Thomas Edison wryly commented "Opportunity is missed by most people because it's dressed in overalls and looks like work". People respond to those with heart, with passion, and who above all are persistent in the face of failure, who work hard for their dreams and don't quit, ever.

The happy news is you need no one's permission, just persistence. Just get up each day, decide precisely what you'll do with those 30 minutes you've committed to marketing yourself and gain real access to the professional communities of Hollywood.

IS THE PAIN OF NOT SUCCEEDING GREAT ENOUGH TO INVEST 30 MINUTES?

As I say in my mastermind, success is a very straightforward discipline. Set aside only 30 minutes every day to put specific, smart strategies to work for you. The cumulative result will be nothing short of a massively successful transformation of your life and career. You'll begin to see concrete results sooner than you think, certainly within a handful of months, but be patient. Your marketing efforts will have a cumulative effect and impact, yielding compound return on your investment of time and effort. The more consistent you are, the more outreach you do on a daily basis, the more consistent your results in the short term and increasingly over time.

This is precisely what I did. All I did really when I was trying to break in to the business. As I built my management business, I did the exact same thing on behalf of each client regardless of whether they were a writer, an actor, or a director. I'd just spend 30 minutes every day for every client, breaking new ground and starting new conversations on their behalf.

Back then, I didn't have a big Rolodex, so I know from experience this is something each of you can do for yourselves. Others will eventually jump on board, but for now I'm only asking you to commit to doing what I've personally done to create success and launch careers time and time again over the years. First for myself, then for many others.

Approach the film and TV business as a *business*. Adopt a regimen of professional habits that would be considered standard for success in any other industry. It's easier to shine in our business than most people believe. Just keep your eye on the prize and don't get overly invested emotionally in any given conversation, opportunity, relationship or circumstance. As Henry Ford said: "Obstacles are those frightful things you see when you take your eyes off your goals."

Be persistent. Be the architect of your own luck. People will jump on board to help, but they want to line up and stand shoulder to shoulder with those who first are willing to aid and abet their own cause.

Perseverance is not a long race; it is many short races one after another.

~ Walter Elliott

So that wraps up your success strategies. You have the techniques, you have the plan, you know what to do, and day by day you'll take action to make that success a reality. So what's left?

A filmmaker's favorite words: That's a Wrap!

THAT'S A WRAP

I love the creative process. I love the people who choose to be our storytellers: you — the writers, producers, directors and actors. My wish for you is great success in whatever creative path you've chosen.

And I believe it's your *obligation* to succeed, because never has our global community been more in need of its storytellers.

> *You do not have the right to eliminate yourself, you do not belong to you. You belong to the universe. The significance of you will forever remain obscure to you, but you may assume that you are fulfilling your significance if you apply yourself to converting all your experience to the highest dvantage of others.*
>
> ~ Buckminster Fuller

What I have attempted to offer in this book are the tactics, habits and specific strategies that provide a crystal clear map to making inroads, gaining access and, ultimately, to *making it* in Hollywood.

Take action and apply the strategies in this book. Devote 30 minutes a day, not for a week or two, but day in and day out for a minimum of a handful of months. Why only a handful? Because by then, you don't need me to remind you. Your results will speak for themselves and drive you to do even more of what I've taught you.

Apply yourself. Get all the education you can, but then, by God, do something. Don't just stand there, make it happen.

~ Lee Iacocca

Your only responsibility is to be accountable, to stay in action, to be strategic and create a daily habit of creating momentum. One step at a time. One moment at a time. Allow that some details will be handled for you, and know that some of those details will forever remain a mystery and only be partially revealed in hindsight. So many of the influences and conversations and participants that support our success are invisible to us, and lead to results we could never predict... but they come into our lives only if we stay in action.

Looking back on my career, I appreciate how much I couldn't know or measure the impact of my choices at the time. But the results were indisputable, the cumulative outcome of repeated, smart, persistent actions and outreach. Some things are beyond serendipity. How could I have known...

- **A 23 year old computer programmer turns out to be J.F. Lawton,** one of the most talented writers I'll ever have the pleasure of collaborating with. Having hired him to program an early Mac computer and spending three weeks working together, our rapport grew to the point he shared his writing with me.
- **If I'd not befriended Michelle Satter** and let her see what drives me, I would never have known about the Sundance Production Lab and *3000* might never have gained the attention of Hollywood, and been produced as *Pretty Woman*.
- **If I'd not networked and met a particular young entertainment attorney,** I'd have missed a major opportunity to discover *The Mothman Prophecies*.
- **If I'd not seen the writers' strike of 1988 as opportunity instead of a problem,** I'd likely not have made a low-budget film and found my way to a whole new career as a producer.

But I couldn't know how any of these things would play out. I just let people know who I am, what excites me, what I'm looking for. The same approach works for us all. It will work for you just the same.

REMIND YOURSELF DAILY

- Find out what people care about and help them get it.
- Ask for advice, not favors.
- When you ask for advice, you gift people the opportunity to know you and to become emotionally connected to you. It's earnest, genuine, powerful.
- When you invest energy into people, you gain emotional equity. Which leads to access – to a person's heart, mind, ideas and contacts. And that access enables you to influence outcomes. That's key to building a strong inner circle and a long-term success.

My realistic goal is 5-10% of those who read this book will be sufficiently motivated to get in gear, do it for real, embrace and execute these tactics. For those who do, I want to hear your stories, and hope you keep me abreast of your progress. It's going to get exciting.

Thanks for reading this book, and for being committed enough to take action, and turn your dreams into your career.

I wish each and every one of you amazing success.

Gary W. Goldstein
BreakingIntoHollywood.com

)

Index

ABOUT THE AUTHOR

GARY W. GOLDSTEIN

Pretty Woman + Under Siege + The Mothman Prophecies

Gary W. Goldstein builds and tells stories.

He has produced some of Hollywood's biggest box-office hits, generating well over One Billion Dollars in worldwide revenue, receiving multiple Academy Award nominations, People's Choice Awards, a Golden Globe and various other honors

Arriving in Hollywood in 1982, Gary created the first ever management firm specializing exclusively in the representation of writers and directors across film and tv. Turning the 1988 Writers Guild of America strike into an opportunity, Gary raised capital and in the course of the coming year produced his first two 'indie' theatrical feature films and caught the producing bug.

Gary next developed and sold to Touchstone Pictures (sister label to Disney) a screenplay by J.F. Lawton, a young unknown writer, a script titled "3000", later to become "Pretty Woman". Able to attract his dream cast, Gary re-developed and co-produced this critically acclaimed film starring Julia Roberts and Richard Gere. Directed by Garry Marshall, Pretty Woman went on to become the highest grossing live-action film in Disney's history, garnering the People's Choice Awards for Best Picture, Best Comedy, Best Actor and Best Actress, as well as both a Golden Globe Award and Oscar Nomination for Julia Roberts.

In addition to the slate of films Gary later produced at various major studios, Gary practiced as an attorney in San Francisco and later served as president of two divisions of IAM.com, an Internet entertainment company successfully funded at $50MM.

Gary's spoken at TEDx, served as Vice Chairman of The Elevision Network, been published by the Huffington Post, was a contributing author for the Napoleon Hill Foundation's newest publication "Stickability", as well as Harper Collin's "The Writer Got Screwed (but didn't have to)".

Gary regularly speaks to creative audiences and has given talks at American Film Institute, UCLA, Emerson College, De Anza College, the Dallas Screenwriters Association, the Screenwriting Conference at Santa Fe, and the Great American Screenwriting Conference, among other groups.

Connect with Gary

BreakingIntoHollywood.com

Google+ Page
http://bit.ly/BIHgplus

Google+ Community
http://bit.ly/BIHcomm

Facebook
https://www.facebook.com/BreakingIntoHllywd

CPSIA information can be obtained at www.ICGtesting.com
Printed in the USA
BVOW05s1644250915

419303BV00003B/125/P

9 780989 715201